Once again, my friend Dr. Charles St
dealing with a problem we all face in
of combining personal experiences, b
able to equip me with the tools and "1 ... ........, ...., ..... over-
come the stressors in my own life . . . and as a husband of twenty-six years, a father of
three girls, a pastor of a growing church, a friend to many, and a son to aging parents,
those stressors real. I have no doubt that *Stress Less* will do the same for you, so be
encouraged and dig in!

**DR. DAVID WHITTEN**, Lead Pastor, Temple Baptist Church, Laurel MS

As a family doctor with over forty years of experience in the exam room, I can state
emphatically the overwhelming impact that stress has upon our physical and emotional well-being. Stress is almost impossible to treat through pharmacological agents
alone . . . it takes behavioral change and insight into its presence in our lives. Dr.
Charles Stone does a masterful job of showing us through his "habitudes" how to
reprogram our lives and diminish our stressors. Through a wonderful presentation of
biblical truths, neuroscience, and practical skills and insights, Dr. Stone defines a life
with stress and how to treat it effectively. If you are anxious at times, and most of us
are . . . it is a must-read.

**DR. JACK C. EVANS**, M.D, FAAFP

Stress is unavoidable, but it doesn't have to be unmanageable. In *Stress Less*, Charles
Stone weaves biblical truth, brain science, and practical tools into a powerful guide
for building resilience. This book is packed with insights that are easy to understand
and even easier to apply. If you're looking for a fresh approach to managing stress and
finding joy, this is the resource you need.

**MAC LAKE**, founder, The Multiply Group, multibook author

Whether you lead in business or in the church, it's essential to prioritize the holistic
flourishing of those you lead. With the heart of a pastor and the insights of a scholar,
Charles Stone offers both a compelling explanation and the motivation needed for
leaders to make building stress resilience a central organizational discipline. *Stress
Less* provides practical, actionable strategies that leaders who care deeply for their
communities can begin prioritizing, modeling, and promoting immediately. In our
current societal context this book is an urgent, must-read for any leader looking to
cultivate a healthier, more resilient culture.

**BRIAN CYGAN**, cofounder and CEO, The Exercise Coach®, America's #1 Largest
Personal Training Organization

Dr. Charles Stone has done it again! He has written a book on emotional and mental
health that addresses the issues so many are dealing with. Stress Less will help you just
like it helped me. Mental, physical, and emotional exhaustion are at an epidemic level.
I know I've personally dealt with it; you likely have as well. Dr. Stone gives us the practical steps needed to regain the strength needed to fulfill our God-given purpose. This
book is a must-have for not only you, but probably several people you know.

**BRIAN DODD**, blogger, Senior Ministry Consultant, INJOY Stewardship
Solutions

*Stress Less*. Charles Stone had me at the title. Of course I want less stress in my life, but telling myself to stop stressing typically only makes me more stressed. In this book, Charles weaves scientific research with biblical insights to provide an invaluable guide for you to live a life with less stress. What a fantastic resource!

**JENNI CATRON**, author, speaker, leadership, and culture strategist

Entertaining, insightful, and important! New perspectives at the intersection of neuroscience, stress, and faith with clear and effective tools in how to stress less!

**DR. HEIDI SUMMERS**, Psychology and Counseling Dept., Regent University

*Stress Less* is a master blend of neuroscience, biblical teaching, and helpful practices that will truly help you understand and manage stress. I am so grateful for Charles Stone Jr. and his ability to take complex principles and make them accessible for everyone. I will be recommending this book to my coaching clients for years to come.

**SEAN NEMECEK**, Ministry Burnout Coach and author of *The Weary Leader's Guide to Burnout: A Journey from Exhaustion to Wholeness*

As church leaders, we are constantly navigating stressful situations, whether in our personal lives or ministry. Dr. Charles Stone's *Stress Less* offers practical, brain-based habits combined with biblical insights to help leaders manage stress and build resilience. His "3-B's" approach—biblical truth, brain insights, and best practices—provides actionable steps that can directly benefit anyone leading in today's high-pressure environments. I highly recommend you pick up copies of this book for your team to help them thrive rather than just survive in ministry!

**RICH BIRCH**, founder, unSeminary

It's a telling reflection of our times that a book like this hits so hard—and is so desperately needed. There's no doubt that the negative effects of stress have reached epidemic levels in our society. We all feel it—me included. What we need is resilience. With his most recent book, *Stress Less*, Dr. Charles Stone steps into this need. Dr. Stone's *Stress Less* is not just a book, but a practical and accessible guide that seamlessly blends insights from neuroscience, timeless truths from Scripture, and evidence-based practices. It's a comprehensive tool that can be applied to all aspects of life in our stress-filled modern world.

**DR. DEVEN K MACDONALD**, PhD, Lead Pastor Berean Baptist Church, Burnsville, MN

Stress. We all have it. The question is: How should we deal with it? Charles writes from the perspective of science-backed research plus deeply devotional "habitudes" to help us deal with and redeem it. That sounds bold, but after a lifetime as a pastor and a PhD dissertation reviewing over five hundred studies on stress, Charles has something interesting and helpful to say in *Stress Less*. Start your Stress Resilience Growth Plan by reading this book and downloading the tools for your life. This will help you spiritually, physically, emotionally, and, of course, with your stress.

**DAVE TRAVIS**, Director Strategic Counsel to Pastors and Church Boards, Generis

9 Habits from the Bible and Brain Science
to Build Resilience and Reduce Anxiety

# stress

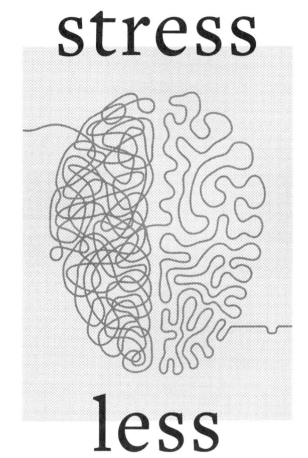

BIBLICALLY SOUND

RESEARCH INFORMED

# less

# CHARLES STONE, PhD

**MOODY PUBLISHERS**
CHICAGO

All Scripture quotations, unless otherwise indicated, are taken from the Holy Bible, New International Version®, NIV®. Copyright ©1973, 1978, 1984, 2011 by Biblica, Inc.™ Used by permission of Zondervan. All rights reserved worldwide. www.zondervan.com The "NIV" and "New International Version" are trademarks registered in the United States Patent and Trademark Office by Biblica, Inc.™

Scripture quotations marked (NLT) are taken from the *Holy Bible*, New Living Translation, copyright © 1996, 2004, 2015 by Tyndale House Foundation. Used by permission of Tyndale House Publishers, Carol Stream, Illinois 60188. All rights reserved.

Scripture quotations marked BBE are taken from the Bible in Basic English, Copyright © 2024, Bible Study Tools. All rights reserved.

Edited by Cheryl Dunlop Molin
Interior design: Puckett Smartt
Cover design: Brittany Schrock
Cover graphic of human brain copyright © 2024 Oleksandr/Adobe Stock (295675731). All rights reserved.

ISBN: 978–0–8024–3351–0

# Contents

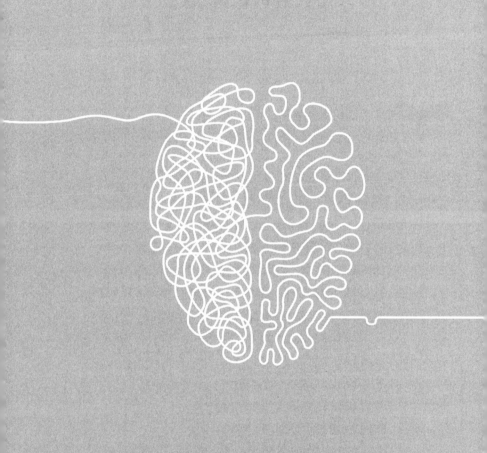

# Introduction

*It's not stress that kills us. It is our reaction to it.*

**HANS SELYE**
*doctor and researcher (1907–82)*

Take this one-question quiz.

Add the parts and find the equation's sum.

Three possible answers follow the quiz.

Here's the equation.

> the Covid pandemic
> + depression
> + cancer surgery
> + a heart irregularity
> + a pre-diabetes diagnosis
> + writing a 500-page PhD dissertation
> _____
>
> = ?????

Here are the answers.

(a) Messy stress.

(b) Mountainous stress.

(c) A messy morass of mountainous stress.

If you chose either a, b, or c, you were correct. The answer to the equation is stress, a messy, mountainous morass of stress.

Even though I eat my broccoli, exercise, take vitamins, and love God, that equation describes what happened to me in an eighteen-month period during the Covid pandemic.

Stress had *overwhelmed me.*

When Covid hit, I was serving a large Canadian church as the lead pastor. After the first cases were diagnosed, the Canadian government prohibited all churches from holding any public services. That forced me to determine how to guide a church of one thousand from my small home office as I stared into a tiny webcam. In the weeks that followed I felt so depressed that my doctor prescribed depression medicine for me.

A few weeks into Covid, tests revealed that prostate cancer had invaded my body. It required out-of-country surgery because wait time for surgery in Canada was unacceptably long.

Another test showed pre-diabetes.

And while on a beach vacation with my wife, I developed an abnormal heartbeat that skyrocketed my heart rate.

Ironically, I was completing a PhD dissertation on . . . stress.

That period in my life does not evoke pleasant memories.

## Stress in America

Perhaps stress looms large in your life . . . a strained relationship, tight finances, or a health issue. Maybe that's why you picked up this book. If you struggle with stress, you are not alone. The American Psychological Society ran polls in 2022 and 2023 called the Stress in America survey.[1] The survey revealed the biggest stressors Americans face. They included personal issues, the effects from the Covid pandemic, political division, crime and violence, racial injustice, and economic concerns. Their surveys also discovered these disturbing statistics:

> 24% of adults rated their average stress between eight and ten (on a scale of one to ten).

45% of adults age 35 to 44 reported a mental health challenge such as depression or anxiety in 2023.

37% said that when they felt stressed, they couldn't bring themselves to do anything about it.

## HOPE AND JOY

Even though we all face stress, God gives us hope we can manage it, bounce back from it, and even become more resilient in response to it.

The Scripture's promises and biblical characters who found victory in stressful circumstances give us hope.

The writings from the fathers of the faith, including Augustine, Aquinas, and Calvin, remind us that all truth is God's truth. The science behind stress resilience also gives us hope we can manage it better.

And evidence-based resilience practices give us hope as we put into practice tools that build stress resilience.

I pray this book will increase your joy as you learn about and use practice tools to build your resilience to stress. In the pages that follow you'll learn nine habits. These practices blend a habit with an attitude. When we apply these practices, with the Holy Spirit's power we can become more resilient to stress and experience the joy that Jesus promises. The Gospel writer John contrasts Satan's purpose with Jesus' purpose when he writes Jesus' words, "The thief's purpose is to steal and kill and destroy. My purpose is to give them a rich and satisfying life" (John 10:10 NLT). Satan will use chronic stress to rob our joy. Jesus, however, desires that the opposite happens. He wants to release His joy into our lives, even during stressful experiences. Growing stress resilience helps us more consistently experience that joy.

## THE THREE B'S

As you read, you'll notice three sources of insight that interweave, much like how the writer of the book of Ecclesiastes applied the word picture a "triple-braided cord" (Eccl. 4:12 NLT) to visualize strength. I call this idea the "3 B's." Each B represents one of these foundational sources: biblical truth, brain insight, and best practices.

The first B, biblical truth, gives the foundation for the book. You'll learn what the writers of the Bible say about stress and life's difficulties. You'll also understand how key biblical characters responded to stressful circumstances. Some responded well. Some didn't. We can learn from them both.

The second B, brain insight, gives a neuroscience perspective on what stress does to the brain, and how changing habits and attitudes can help keep our brains and our bodies healthy. One study on college students found that when we learn about new subjects through a neuroscience lens, it makes that subject more interesting.[2] So you may find your interest in stress resilience enhanced simply because I explain concepts through a neuroscience lens.

The third B, best practices, gets very practical and comes from my and others' research on stress resilience. You'll learn new skills that can enhance your stress resilience, all backed by the current evidence-based research on habits and attitudes proven to work. The following key insight I discovered in my research reinforces why we need to understand stress and how it works. I found that greater knowledge of how to manage stress led to decreased perceived stress, increased resilience, decreased emotional exhaustion, and increased satisfaction.

## THE RESEARCH IN BRIEF

My PhD research involved consulting more than five hundred research studies, articles, and books on stress resilience. I also studied more than four hundred ministry leaders by using surveys, interviews, and so-phisticated computer programs that analyzed that data. From that research came a course on stress resilience that I taught to a group of those leaders.

After the course, I wanted to determine how it helped increase stress resilience among the participants. It helped several stress resilience factors. This book includes insight from the research. The research also yielded interesting findings about how sleep, spiritual practices, and specific skills influence stress resilience. You'll read about those later.

During my PhD research I received two certifications on stress resilience. I must be a glutton for punishment.

My personal life experiences, certifications, and the surprising insight I learned from my PhD research spurred me to write this book to help readers become more resilient to stress. And although neuroscience provides one strand in the three Bs, I won't use heady language. You might even want to learn more about the brain after reading this book.

## Book Organization

Sprinkled throughout the book are suggestions for you to download free tools available at www.charlesstone.com/stress. These will give you further insight and practical help. As you continue through the book, I will encourage you to build your own Stress Resilience Growth Plan to internalize and apply your insights. This plan will include the habits and attitudes that fit your personality and unique situation to best help you grow your resilience. Starting with the practices section, as you go through each chapter, downloadable tools on that practice will help you develop your personalized Stress Resilience Growth Plan.

I divide the book into two sections. Part one (chapters 1–3) lays the groundwork. In it you'll learn what stress is, how it harms your body and brain, three sources of stress, and types of stress. It will highlight how to distinguish between stress management (which looks backward) and resilience (which looks forward). It includes a biblical overview on stress and more research that supports the ideas presented. Finally, you'll discover key factors that form stress resilience, the benefits from resilience, and a key word picture that describes resilience: the rock, egg, tennis ball metaphor.

Part two (chapters 4–12) unpacks the nine practices. With the book's goal to grow stress resilience, these nine practices become the means to that end. Each practice chapter follows the "3 B's" sequence, first a biblical truth and/or an example of a biblical character, then the brain science, and then the best practice/skill for that practice.

At the end of each chapter, you'll find both links to downloadable tools to help you grow that practice and discussion questions to drive the insights deeper. Some questions will relate to your thoughts and emotions. Some will relate to your relationships. And some will relate to your walk with God.

If stress seems to overwhelm you sometimes, you'll find biblical hope and practical help within these pages.

PART 1:

# The Groundwork

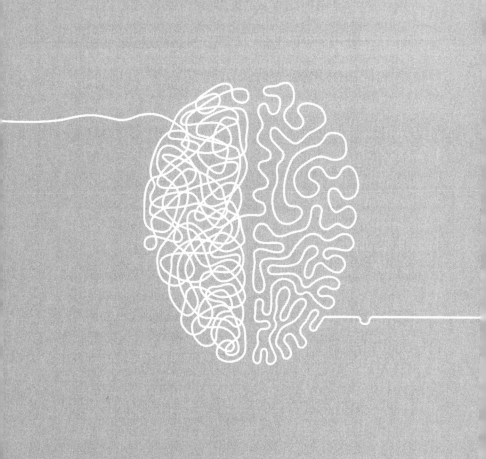

# 1

# What Stress Is

*Stress is the trash of modern life—*
*we all generate it, but if you don't dispose of it properly,*
*it will pile up and overtake your life.*

**DANZAE PACE**

n late 2019, a strange virus began to afflict millions in China. I'm a news junkie, so I followed the story daily (or more like hourly). The year prior, my wife, Sherryl, and I had scheduled a vacation to Jamaica for February 2020. As we get older, we plan to take one nice trip each year until our bones get so creaky that we can't travel anymore.

When we arrived in Jamaica, everything seemed perfect, except one issue. The resort provided free Wi-Fi everywhere—not good for a news junkie on vacation. I couldn't restrain myself and followed the unfolding story online.

News outlets began to report increased Covid shutdowns in many countries. I told my wife that I believed the Canadian government might soon shut down churches. That thought gave me stress because I knew that as a pastor, closing our church would bring significant stress-fueling uncertainty not only to me, but to the congregation as well. Closure would hinder our ability to serve the church and limit the congregation's ability to experience the growth and joy that comes when we gather to worship each week.

We enjoyed our vacation and after a week we flew back home to Canada into Pearson Airport in Toronto. Since the terminal for the airline didn't connect to the main one, the airline provided a bus that ferried us back to the major terminal that housed the luggage carousel.

However, something felt odd during this five-minute ride to the terminal. In hushed tones, people kept whispering the phrase "toilet paper." I soon found out why. I checked the news on my iPhone and learned that the Canadian government had announced a massive nationwide shutdown of everything except essential services. That announcement created a rush on toilet paper. Those quiet conversations? Toilet paper was MIA. Grocery stores' limited supplies dwindled. My thoughts about no toilet paper added another layer of stress.

After we gathered our luggage and loaded our car, we drove to the nearest grocery store. I walked/ran through the store to the paper goods aisle and hoped I didn't telegraph to other customers what I was doing. As I rounded the corner, there it sat at the end of the aisle: one last six-pack of toilet paper. Since I ran track in high school, I immediately put that skill to use. I sprinted down the aisle and snatched it from the shelf. Crisis averted. We had our toilet paper. I felt happy.

The next day, our city became a ghost town because the government had shut down everything except services deemed essential. Now I was forced to lead a church of one thousand through a tiny webcam in my home office. I felt afraid, very afraid. I told myself (or maybe I told God), "I didn't sign up for this." My last few years in ministry were ending, and I had planned a smooth retirement. I didn't expect a pandemic to get in the way. I realized my plans would soon change. Church income dropped dramatically. We slashed the budget and cut salaries. I wondered if we could survive as the church we once were.

More stress.

During those first months we shut down, an anxiety-filled hole grew in my soul as I pondered our church's uncertain future. In one sense, those uncomfortable feelings were normal because the brain doesn't like uncertainty. When we experience uncertainty, the brain evokes the stress response, as it did in me. However, because I stayed in a stress state, I fell into a depression. After I consulted my doctor, he prescribed a depression medicine called an SSRI (selective serotonin reuptake inhibitor, think Prozac). An SSRI drug helps regulate one of our feel-good neurotransmitters (brain chemicals) called serotonin. Over the next six months, the drug helped pull me out of my depression as I led our staff to minister virtually.

My stress began to abate.

About that time, after a regular blood test, my doctor noticed an increasing blood level in a marker that could indicate prostate cancer. After an appointment with a specialist and a later biopsy, the diagnosis confirmed my fears. I had cancer. Boom! Stress spiked again. Ironically, a few months prior, I had begun my PhD studies on stress resilience. I thought, "Maybe these experiences will bring a human touch to my research." However, I didn't plan to become a lab rat.

The surgery went well, and today I am cancer free.

A few months after my surgery, I scheduled our next annual vacation for the following February. This time, we took a cruise to the Caribbean. The ship we chose sparkled with newness. The scrumptious buffets tantalized our palates. (I love buffets.) And the white beaches we visited highlighted the blue Caribbean waters. We planned to relax and de-stress.

At one of the island stops, we splurged and bought an excursion to a well-known beach. It included transportation, lunch, and beach chairs with an umbrella to protect us from the sun. That morning, an intense workout in the ship's gym had overheated my body. Later, after the bus took us to the beach, we discovered that the other guests had taken all the umbrellas. That forced us to bake in our beach chairs with nothing to block the scorching sun.

About an hour into our stay, I felt lightheaded and could barely walk. I dragged my chair to a tiny shady spot beneath a palm tree. My heart felt like it was trying to jump out of my chest. I then remembered that my smartwatch could detect an irregular heartbeat. So I took several measurements. My heart rate was bouncing all over the place. I was experiencing what is called an A-fib episode, short for atrial fibrillation, an irregular heartbeat. I didn't know if that would lead to a heart attack. If I had a heart attack, the island's limited medical facilities wouldn't help much. I told my wife, and she quickly found the excursion guide. The guide then found a wheelchair and wheeled me back to the bus and then onto the ship, where the ship's doctor examined me. By then, my heart rate had dropped back to normal.

Over the next two months, cardiologists performed extensive tests. So far, all the tests show that my heart is in good shape. But that experience had placed another layer of stress on me. I often have wondered if another heart episode lay just around the corner. Besides that experience, another blood test revealed I had pre-diabetes.

So, over an eighteen-month period, I faced stress from multiple directions—my health, my pastoral leadership during the Covid lockdown, and my doctoral project. Before that stress trifecta hit, I had coped well with the normal day-to-day stresses most people face. Those circumstances, however, reminded me to prioritize stress resilience as I aged.

In retrospect, I now see God's hand at work through those difficulties. Those ordeals helped me approach my PhD research on stress resilience at a different level, not just as a sterile researcher removed from life, but as a fellow struggler.

## What Is Stress?

None of us can insulate ourselves from stressful situations. We all deal with regular stress. You may care for a chronically ill family member, with no end in sight. A health issue or pain may nag you. You may experience prejudice due to your skin color or accent. You may work in a stressful job with few prospects for a better one. Inflation may have placed your finances in a precarious position. A difficult marriage or relationship may weigh you down. A deep loss may have thrown you into an emotional hole. Political polarization may gnaw at you.

Stress is inevitable.

We often can do little about the circumstances that cause it. Yet a commitment to grow resilience gives us hope as we apply the proven stress-reduction skills explained in this book. Stress need not bury us or bleed us dry. We can learn from it. And with new skills and insight, we can grow through it.

As you read this book, it's crucial to lay a foundation for stress, because all new learning is based on prior learning.[1] As you understand some basic brain-based knowledge, the specific practices will make more sense, will stick better in your memory, and will help you use them effectively. So, in this chapter and the next two, you'll learn some brain basics, how to define and contrast stress and resilience, and what each does to the body and brain. You'll also understand what causes stress and what Scripture tells us about it. These insights will provide a strong objective foundation as you create your personal Stress Resilience Growth Plan and apply the nine practices.

## A BIT OF HISTORY ABOUT STRESS RESEARCH

In the 1930s, Hungarian endocrinologist Hans Selye developed the modern theory of stress as a response. Whereas Selye highlighted the stress response, Western researchers focused on the stimulus, the issue that caused the stress response.[2] In the late 1960s and early 1970s, psychiatrists Thomas Holmes and Richard Rahe developed a scale of forty-one stressful life events, called the Holmes-Rahe Stress Inventory. It included major life stressors such as the "death of a spouse, divorce, incarceration, severe illness, and being fired." It also "included positive events like getting married, vacations, and retirement."[3]

One researcher found that stress created a dynamic relationship between people and their environment. How they appraised the situation influenced their coping skills. He found that ordinary life events might do more harm than major life events. He wrote, "The seemingly little things that irritate and upset people, such as one's dog throwing up on the living room rug, delays in the commute to work, having too many responsibilities, being lonely, having an argument with one's spouse, may get out of hand."[4] Their research found that not only do harsh life events (like my cancer) cause stress, but the small daily life stuff that accumulates over time (like your computer constantly crashing) does as well.

Finally, although we can't avoid many stressful situations that life brings us, we can respond to them in ways that strengthen our walk with God and protect our physical, emotional, mental, and relational health. That's what these practices can help you do.

## THREE CAUTIONS

As we delve deeper into stress resilience and how to grow it, consider these three cautions.

First, avoid an unhealthy response to chronic stress called stress avoidance. When we try to avoid stress, it can generate even more stress. Health psychologist Kelly M. McGonigal, PhD, writes this about stress avoidance:

> It's the ironic consequence of trying to avoid stress: You end up creating more sources of stress while depleting the resources that should be supporting you. As the stress piles up, you become increasingly overwhelmed and isolated, and therefore even more likely to rely on avoidant coping strategies, like trying to steer clear of stressful situations or to escape your feelings with self-destructive distractions. The more firmly

committed you are to avoiding stress, the more likely you are to find yourself in this downward spiral.[5]

Second, don't expect a cure-all, a magic wand to zap away your stress and its effects. However, as you read *Stress Less,* plan to learn new skills and attitudes that can help you minimize your stress reactions and grow your resilience.

For example, when we regulate our emotions (Practice 2: Reveal How You Feel), we increase cognitive flexibility, the ability to keep options open in stressful situations. When we reappraise stressful situations in a more positive way (Practice 4: Audit Your Thoughts), we can calm our fear center and think more clearly. Sleep and exercise (Practice 9: Sleep Smart) can put us into a better mood to handle stress and help release the brain's fertilizer, called BDNF (brain derived neurotrophic factor). And optimism (Practice 6: Cultivate Certainty) and gratitude (Practice 7: Grow Gratitude) foster better relationships, which can lead to a safe relationship environment (Practice 8: Safeguard Safety), all significant skills that build resilience.[6]

Third, avoid using stress-resilience development just as a tool to help you feel better. If we approach resilience in a self-centered way, we'll become selfish, and growing our stress resilience will become all about us and our needs. Although we must take care of ourselves by managing stress, we also must serve others. That often requires sacrifice and stepping into stressful situations. However, research tells us that when we serve others and become more cognizant of their needs (called pro-social behavior), we actually feel better.

## FOUNDATIONS FIRST

You might wonder why learning about the brain enhances stress resilience. Should you just skip those parts and go directly to the practices? You could, but if you did, you'd lose the positive benefits from a relatively new field called neuroscience pain education (NPE). NPE proposes that as we understand how the brain processes pain, we not only can manage physical pain better, but we can also manage social and emotional pain better. Physical, social, and emotional pain all cause stress. Multiple studies on patients with chronic pain[7] show that when they learned how the brain processed pain, outcomes improved and stress decreased.[8]

Researchers have also found that social and emotional pain engage the same brain circuits as physical pain. Learning about these brain processes can moderate the emotional and social pain associated with stress.[9] So, when we learn about the brain and stress resilience, we grow our resilience.

One of the leading experts on resilience, Dr. Amit Sood, affirms this idea about brain education. He developed a stress reduction program at the Mayo Clinic called SMART, Stress Management and Resiliency Training.[10] He designed this research-backed program around three key concepts: awareness, attention, and attitude. As we understand these concepts,[11] we can build resilience.

Building stress resilience does for our brains what physical exercise does for our hearts. When we don't train our hearts through exercise, our heart muscles fatigue more easily. In the same way, not training our brains (like learning how it works) may cause more mental fatigue and less of the cognitive reserve we need to manage stress. When we learn how our brains work, however, we build a more resilient one. As we learn more about our brains, stress, and resilience, we will gain a good foundation to apply resilience to stressful situations. Below, I give more detail about how the brain works when we experience stress.

## THE TWO FLAVORS OF STRESS: ACUTE AND CHRONIC

We need not view stress as a big bad wolf, because not all stress is bad. God designed our bodies and brains to experience it. Researchers have found an upside to some kinds of stress.[12] Healthy stress increases focus. It can help us become more social as we connect with others. It can enhance learning as we replay a stressful situation in our minds to make sense of it and learn from it so that we can better handle a similar situation in the future. Learning from stressful experiences is a resilience trait.

Neither should we view stress as poles of a single continuum from bad (threat/distress) to good (challenge/eustress). Rather, both challenge and threat can occur in a single event. For any given stressful experience, both a positive and a negative response can simultaneously occur. When we appraise an event negatively, we see it as a threat, a bad thing. When we appraise an event positively, called eustress, we can see it as a challenge, a good thing. "Eustress reflects the extent to which cognitive appraisal of a situation or event is seen to either benefit an individual or enhance his or her well-being."[13]

For example, let's say on your way to work you wreck your car. No one gets hurt, but you total your car. During the few seconds leading up to and during your accident, hormones and neurotransmitters flood your brain and body and you experience significant stress. Yet as time passes, the stress chemicals in your bloodstream and brain dissipate. As a result, you will think more clearly to reappraise the situation and to tell yourself something like this (if you are well-insured): "This is bad, but I needed a new car, anyway. This gives me a good excuse to get one." So, although you initially felt threatened (you could have gotten hurt and your stress chemicals skyrocketed), you also felt challenged (it's not all bad because you get to pick out a new car). We'll learn more about the power of reappraisal later.

We experience acute stress, also called transient stress, when stressful conditions pass rather quickly. Educators Oakley, Rogowsky, and Sejnowski write, "Transient stress releases hormones such as adrenaline and cortisol in the brain. In moderate amounts, these molecules enhance the connections between neurons—almost like greasing a pan to prevent fried potatoes from sticking to the bottom."[14]

In fact, acute stress can improve our performance without harming our bodies or brains. It motivates us to action to get things done, meet deadlines, focus on a task, pay attention in class, and react quickly in a threatening situation (like slamming on your brakes to avoid a wreck). Although a life situation may instantly evoke the stress response, our stress levels will usually return to baseline after the event. God created us this way so that we could survive when threatened.

However, chronic stress is the big bad wolf. Chronic stress means stress caused by unremitting threatening conditions and events (real or imagined) when we are on high alert for long periods of time. It creates distress, which causes negative thoughts, memories, and emotions, as well as negative body and brain effects, to stick with us longer. It also lowers our tolerance to normal stress events that we usually could process well. "Too much stress, even if it's just transient, changes the effects of the hormonal oil. Instead of greasing the connections, the excess stress causes neural connections to burn and stick, so nothing flows."[15]

Scripture says much about stress and its effects. Each chapter that follows includes insight from Scripture about stress, its effects, and its solution. Below, I introduce what Scripture says about the subject.

## What Does the Bible Say About Stress?

Humanity has experienced stress since the fall. Many key figures in the Bible experienced it, including Elijah, Jonah, Esther, David, Peter, Martha, Paul, and Jesus Himself. Even though the word itself does not appear in the Scriptures, similar words describe the idea. Words such as trials, tribulations, troubles, hardships, ordeals, difficulties, distress, persecution, affliction, suffering, adversity, pressure, disaster, and discipline mirror the idea behind stress.[16] We must frame it within a biblical perspective to best deal with it.

The chapters that follow describe the nine practices and how to use them. You'll see how key figures in the Bible responded to stress. And as you learn about stress resilience, it's important to anchor your understanding in God's Word.

Unhealthy stress responses that engage the brain's emotional accelerator (the sympathetic nervous system, more on that later) were consequences of the fall. Perhaps God initially wired Adam and Eve's stress circuits to only respond to pleasurable experiences that evoked good stress (eustress).

We experience positive emotions from eustress, for example, when we feel challenged to complete a task at work and finish it well. Such a task may have challenged us, but responding to the challenge satisfied us because completing a task evokes the release of dopamine, one of the brain's "feel good" chemicals, into our brains.

Although Adam and Eve felt the challenge to care for the garden, they experienced no threat to their safety. So they didn't need any brain circuits to initiate the fight-or-flight response. Yet after the fall everything changed. The fall apparently rewired their brain circuits or brought to life existing survival circuits that lay dormant prior to the fall. As a result, sin in Adam's and Eve's hearts now evoked new stressful emotions—fear and guilt—and they hid from God.

Stressful difficulties and tests in life give us opportunities to rewire those damaged threat circuits we inherited from Adam and Eve. When we apply the practices, respond to stress in God-honoring ways, and yield to the Holy Spirit's direction in the moment, God will change our brain circuits to better match their original intended purpose prior to the fall.

Human flourishing, a meta-theme in the Bible, describes God's purpose for us. Jesus calls it the abundant life. Seminary professor and human flourishing expert Dr. Jonathan Pennington says that our goal in following Jesus is to glorify God and to experience human flourishing ourselves, but also to promote it. Resilience not only evidences human flourishing but develops it as well. He writes,

> Our theological reflections and their practical outworking must be to bring true human flourishing [and resilience] to individuals and society as a whole. This must be motivated, informed, and colored by the reality of God's coming kingdom, centered on Jesus the Son, and empowered by the Holy Spirit. Without this anchoring, the pursuit of human flourishing is not biblical. But this spiritual understanding does not make it less physical and practical. . . . At its core and in its very essence, God's saving work, his redemptive activity, his goal for humanity and all creation is precisely this: that we flourish fully even as he himself flourishes perfectly, completely, and with overflowing abundance. We should cease thinking of spirituality and godliness as something that has nothing to do with human well-being and flourishing, including in a physical, economic, psychological, and relational sense.[17]

God wants us to experience the abundant life, human flourishing, and personal well-being, of which resilience composes a major part. Peter reflected this when he wrote, "His divine power has given us everything we need for a godly life through our knowledge of him who called us by his own glory and goodness" (2 Peter 1:3). Peter (and Dr. Pennington) explain that stress resilience must be Christ-centric. And one way we release God's power in our lives is to wisely steward our bodies and brains by handling stress better. We handle stress better when we grow our resilience to it.

The Scriptures place a high value on our bodies, and by inference, our brains, since they are part of our bodies. The clearest arguments on body care come from the apostle Paul. He used the human body as a metaphor. He called the church the body of Christ (Eph. 1:22–23). He described spiritual gifts by using a body as a metaphor (1 Cor. 12). He told us to "offer your bodies as a living sacrifice" (Rom. 12:1).

He even describes our bodies as temples of the Holy Spirit. "Do you not know that your bodies are temples of the Holy Spirit . . . ?" (1 Cor. 6:19). In verse 20, he commands us to "honor God with your bodies." These words *honor, temple,* and *sacrifice* reinforce our responsibility to make wise choices to keep our bodies (and brains) healthy. These choices also include other habits like eating a good diet and regular exercise.

However, we must add to that healthy habit list this one: growing our stress resilience. God gave us a human body for life on earth (and we get a new one in heaven), and since our bodies matter to God, they should matter to us as well. As we learn to respond to chronic stress with resilience and lessen the negative effects from stress, we show we care for our bodies. When our bodies and brains work better because we have responded in healthy ways to stress, we can serve God more effectively, love others more consistently, and grow our faith most optimally.

Dr. Wayne Oates (1917–99), a psychologist and religious educator, coined the word "workaholic" and paved the way for the modern pastoral care movement. He wrote extensively on stress and burnout and emphasized that stress management requires us to examine our assumptions about faith, ourselves, and God. He is one of the few who developed a theology or biblical framework of stress. I summarize his ideas below.[18]

Oates wrote that certain concepts and words (tribulation, faith development, burden, testing, temptation) give a biblical interpretation of stress.

1. **Stress as it relates to the word *tribulation*.** Jesus and Paul both spoke about the tribulation and difficulty we will face in this world (see John 16:33; Rom. 5:3-4; James 1:2-4).

2. **Stress as it relates to faith development.** Oates writes we should view stress as developmental, and if we avoid it or ignore these teachable opportunities to grow our faith, they will accumulate into "distress." He wrote, "Faith means having the courage to move through times of stress without shrinking back."[19]

3. **Stress as it relates to the word *burden*.** Paul uses this word in Galatians 6:2 when he tells us, "Carry each other's burdens." Oates writes, "The word *responsibility* is a good synonym for both the biblical word *burden* and the contemporary word *stress*."[20]

4. **Stress as it relates to the words *testing* and *temptation*.** The word *peirasmos* means trial, test, or temptation. Satan can use stressful experiences to draw us into sin, whereas God allows them as opportunities to further develop our resilience. Oates writes that stress is the "forge in which our real theology is hammered out."[21]

Ultimately, stress events fit within God's eternal plan that weaves eternal meaning into our lives. Oates counsels us to "put personal stresses into the context of the sovereignty of God, the redemptive participation of Jesus Christ, and the Presence of God in Christ in the Holy Spirit."[22]

In the next chapter, we'll continue to build the groundwork for stress resilience as we consider these topics: how the brain's stress response works, how stress harms our bodies and brains, signs of burnout, and how stress management differs from resilience.

## APPLICATION

1. In what ways do you resonate with my stress experiences?

2. How would you describe your current stress experience, acute or chronic? Why?

3. How could you honor God if you strengthen your resilience to stress?

4. What one commitment about developing stress resilience could you make to yourself and to the Lord?

5. Write it down and post it where you will see it for the next seven days.

For downloadable tools, visit this web link: www.charlesstone.com/stress.

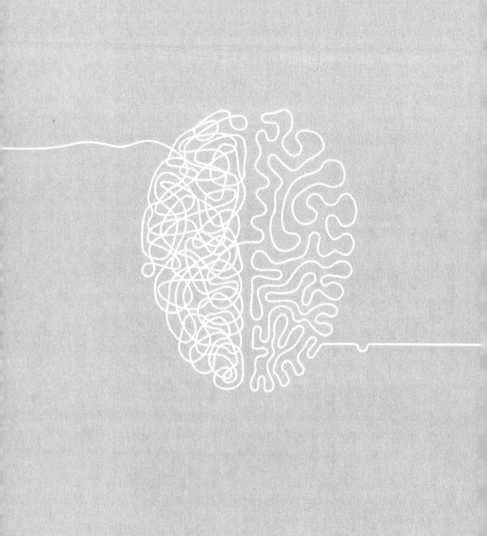

# 2

# What Stress Does

*The greatest weapon against stress*
*is our ability to choose one thought over another.*

**WILLIAM JAMES**
*American philosopher and psychologist (1842–1910)*

You'll recall in the prior chapter I distinguished chronic stress from acute stress. Acute stress comes and goes. Your car breaks down, which stresses you for a few hours, but you get it fixed without too much damage to your bank account. After a few hours (or a day or so), your body, brain, and emotions come back into balance (called homeostasis).

However, if you drive a clunker and don't have the cash to replace it, you might experience chronic stress if repeated breakdowns continue to drain your bank account. And your response to chronic stress harms your body, brain, relationships, and walk with God.

This chapter focuses on what stress does to us, specifically what the harmful kind, chronic stress, does. In the pages that follow you'll read about these facets related to chronic stress:

- What stress feels like, from the pen of King David
- A brief primer on the stress response
- The body's adaptive response to stress: homeostasis and allostasis
- The three primary sources of stress

- The negative effects from stress
- The ultimate result from chronic stress: burnout

## King David and Stress

Kind David penned many psalms that reflected deep and painful emotions he experienced in his life. Psalm 31 describes these emotions when his son Absalom tried to usurp his throne, a four-year relationship conflict that ended with Absalom's untimely death. As you read this psalm, look for words David used to describe how he felt through this chronically stressful experience. Ask yourself if you can identify with how he felt when you've faced stress.

> In you, LORD, I have taken refuge; let me never be put to shame; deliver me in your righteousness. Turn your ear to me, come quickly to my rescue; be my rock of refuge, a strong fortress to save me. Since you are my rock and my fortress, for the sake of your name lead and guide me. (vv. 1–3)

He begins this psalm as he describes God as his *rock* and *fortress*, his place of safety and refuge whom he turns to in this stressful circumstance. He conveys a sense of urgency when he writes, "Come quickly to my rescue." I've put in italics the stress-related words he uses.

> Keep me from the *trap* that is set for me, for you are my refuge. Into your hands I commit my spirit. (vv. 4–5)

This situation was so difficult, treacherous, and stressful that he called it a *trap*.

> I will be glad and rejoice in your love, for you saw my *affliction* and knew the *anguish* of my soul. (v. 7)

His experience created anguish, yet he still trusted in a loving God when he wrote, "Into your hands I commit my spirit," the words Jesus quoted just before He died as He hung on the cross. Here, David reminds us that God knows what creates stress in our lives. God sees our affliction.

> You have not given me into the hands of the enemy but have set my feet in a spacious place. (v. 8)

He now expects God's future deliverance into what he calls a *spacious place*. His flood of confidence then gives way to reality. His anguish fueled by a rebellious son almost defies description. He cries out with words that describe what chronic stress can feel like.

> Be merciful to me, Lord, for I am in *distress*; my eyes grow *weak* with *sorrow*, my soul and body with *grief*. My life is consumed by *anguish* and my years by *groaning*; my *strength fails* because of my *affliction*, and my bones grow *weak*. Because of all my enemies, I am the utter *contempt* of my neighbors and an object of *dread* to my closest friends—those who see me on the street *flee* from me. I am *forgotten* as though I were *dead*; I have become like *broken pottery*. For I hear many whispering, "*Terror* on every side!" They *conspire* against me and *plot* to take my life. (vv. 9–13)

He describes how stress has affected his health. His *strength had failed*. He felt *contempt from others*. Distress *filled his soul*. His desperation mirrors how stress can make us feel: distressed, weak, sorrowful, grieved, anguished, groaning, afflicted, held in contempt and forgotten by others, broken, terrorized, and even conspired against.

David felt hopeless, even to the point of death ("they . . . plot to take my life"). Although this chapter describes what chronic stress can do to us if we don't respond positively, the chapters that follow give hope and practical tools to grow our resilience to it. When we apply these tools, we can triumph over the effects from chronic stress, as did David.

After he describes how he felt, he comes full circle at the end of the chapter and reminds himself that God will sustain him.

But I trust in you, LORD; I say, "You are my God." (v. 14)

The phrase, *my God*, expressed endearment, trust, and closeness. In the remaining verses he wrote about God's unfailing love, His sovereign control, and His goodness.

However, David admits that in his human frailty he had doubted God and lost perspective. He wrote "in my alarm" in verse 22 to describe how he had overstated the problem and understated God's plan and provision when Absalom rebelled. We often do that as well.

He ends with these encouraging words:

Love the LORD, all his faithful people! The LORD preserves those who are true to him, but the proud he pays back in full. Be strong and take heart, all you who hope in the LORD. (vv. 23–24)

He reminds us to persevere (develop resilience) regardless of the circumstances. He believed that God ultimately controls every circumstance. Written from David's personal experience, this psalm pictures how chronically stressful circumstances affect us. It also reminds us that God gives us the ability to grow from and through our stress with perspective change, which enhances resilience. The next chapters give practical, biblical, evidence-based practices to build resilience.

## A Brief Primer on the Stress Response

Chronic stress, the kind that keeps us on high alert for long periods of time (in contrast to acute stress, which lasts a short time), harms both body and brain. Seven in ten Americans suffer from some physical problem related to it.[1] Stress-related issues account for more than 60 percent of doctor visits.[2] These problems include heart and gastrointestinal issues. Other health issues come from a compromised immune system, another effect from chronic stress.[3]

Chronic stress also shrinks parts of the brain, specifically memory areas.[4] Simultaneously, it fosters growth in the amygdala,[5] which creates the fear response. Unhealthy thinking and emotional and behavioral choices in response to stressful situations can magnify the damage stress causes. In the next chapter we'll look at what stress does to the brain and body.

Several cross-connected parts of the brain are involved in the stress response, including the insula, the amygdala, the cingulate, the pre-frontal cortex, and the hippocampus.[6] There are two of almost every part of your brain, but when I refer to a brain part, I will use the conventional singular form.

The insula, a prune-sized collection of brain cells (neurons) deep within our brain, makes us aware of our internal body states and feelings like trust, empathy, guilt, and disgust.[7] It's involved in giving us our "gut feelings."[8] I believe the Holy Spirit often engages this part of our brain through intuition about ourselves and others.

The anterior cingulate is a part of the brain behind our forehead that always looks for threatening situations and is involved in pain processing. It's like a smoke alarm in our houses. As a smoke alarm alerts us to dangerous smoke, so the cingulate alerts us to a potential survival threat.

The almond-shaped amygdala (a component of the "feel-y" part of the brain) kick-starts the stress response and tags memories connected to emotion.[9] Think of an imaginary neural pink sticky note attached to an emotional memory in your brain, perhaps a time in the first grade when you felt deeply embarrassed. The amygdala allows you to recall and relive that negative emotional moment and feel those same emotions even decades later. It also tags positive memories. We recall negative emotional experiences more often and more quickly than positive ones because negative emotions create bigger and brighter neural sticky notes.

Some have described this process by saying that *bad (emotion) is stronger than good (emotion).*[10] More neural pathways travel from the amygdala to the front part of the brain, the pre-frontal cortex (the "think-y" part of the brain) than vice versa. And its central location gives it the proximity to quickly influence the body's stress response, operating five times faster than the pre-frontal cortex.[11] This gives it an unfair advantage in a reason-versus-emotion tug-of-war.

The amygdala is quick at feeling yet poor at making accurate judgments. Your brain's feeler can even incite anxiety through unconscious associations in your memory, rather than relying on logic.

The part of the brain highly involved in memory is the hippocampus, a seahorse-shaped collection of brain cells. This part of the brain stores and processes short-term memories and helps turn them into long-term memories (a process called consolidation).

The body's wiring, the nervous system, divides into three key systems. The first two are the central nervous system (the brain and spinal cord) and the peripheral nervous system (the nerves that flow from the spinal cord). Within this system lies the autonomic nervous system, which is involved in the innervation of such body parts as the heart, lungs, smooth muscles, and glands. It includes three distinct divisions, two of which are especially involved in the stress response: the brain's emotional accelerator (the sympathetic nervous system) and the brain's emotional brake (the parasympathetic nervous system).

The third component of the peripheral nervous system, the enteric nervous system, is involved in gastrointestinal function. Stress affects it as well, like when we get a stomachache.

The sympathetic nervous system creates what we might dub "emotional fires," and the parasympathetic nervous system, when activated, "puts them out." They work in tandem like a seesaw. When the sympathetic nervous system revs up too much and for too long (chronic stress), problems ensue.

The poly-vagal theory proposes that another component of the peripheral nervous system also plays a role in the stress response, alongside these other two systems.[12] This component can cause a person to freeze in a stressful situation. One component can also foster warm and trusting relationships.

When the brain senses danger, whether real (a bear is chasing you) or imagined (your boss acts like a bear), the amygdala takes notice. It quickly signals the sympathetic nervous system to snap to. This is called the SAM (sympathetic-adrenal-medullary) system. "It activates fast, like 911. Its primary arsenal is adrenaline and related hormones. They lock on the receptors of many organs—heart, lungs, liver, muscles, endocrine glands, and immune system—to immediately start the stress/survival response."[13]

This system and the resultant emotions can weaken the thinking part of the brain and impair clear thinking. Below I've listed several physiological changes that happen in our bodies and brains when stress activates the sympathetic nervous system. These occur without our intentional effort.

1. Our brain releases chemicals (neurotransmitters and hormones) into our brain and blood so we can fight or flee. It increases our attention and shunts blood from less essential areas, like our skin, to more crucial ones, like our muscles (to help us run from that bear).

2. Our heart beats faster and blood pressure rises to send more blood to our muscles for the same reason, to fight or flee danger, or even freeze (like when a deer freezes when it sees headlights at night).

3. Breathing increases so that more oxygen flows into our brain to maximize alertness and attention.

4. It temporarily enhances hearing and vision so we can see and hear better (to fight or flee the bear).

5. Non-crucial systems (digestion, saliva glands, etc.) slow down or stop so that the important body parts like the heart and muscular systems receive more blood and energy.

6. We may get goosebumps, a dry mouth, sweat, or feel we need to go the bathroom right then.

7. It puts our brain's emotional system (the limbic system) on highest alert. It gets supercharged, which can fuel defensiveness or reactivity.

8. As our negative emotions strengthen from acute stress, they compromise the "think-y" part of our brain (the pre-frontal cortex). We won't think as clearly unless we draw upon our stress-resilience reservoir. Speed is king here. We want to slam the door without deliberating, "Should I close the door to keep out this bear?"

The second step of the stress response occurs when a stressor does not quickly end. Another brain system starts what we can visualize as three dominoes standing on end next to each other. When one domino falls, it makes another one fall, which makes the third one fall. This system is called the HPA-axis, an acronym for three other parts of the brain that work together in the stress response: the hypothalamus, the pituitary gland, and the adrenal glands. If the actual or perceived threat continues, this system kicks in.

Chemicals cascade down from one of these brain parts to the next (one domino causes the next one to fall) and finally to the adrenal glands atop the kidneys. These glands release what is called the stress hormone, cortisol, into the bloodstream.

Cortisol helps the body maintain steady supplies of blood sugar for fuel and quick energy. It keeps the body in the fight-or-flight mode when threatened. When a threat passes, the brain's brake (parasympathetic nervous system) dampens the stress response started by the brain's accelerator (the sympathetic nervous system). It puts the fire out and we feel greater calm. Scientists call this state homeostasis, when the body's systems are in balance.

That's what happens to our bodies when stressed. God wired our bodies and brains in this way to deal with life's challenges. Problems arise when we stay stuck in stress with unhealthy levels of cortisol coursing through our bodies. When our stress response system is on for an extended period, this chronic stress can harm our bodies and brains, hurt relationships, hinder clear thinking and emotional control, and diminish our job effectiveness.

Stress can rob us of human flourishing, the joy Jesus promises in John 15:11: "I have told you this so that my joy may be in you and that your joy may be complete."[14]

## The Body's Stress Balance Process: Homeostasis and Allostasis

Although stress can harm us at multiple levels, God designed our brains with a system that helps us adapt—homeostasis. Acting much like a thermostat, homeostasis adjusts to the environment to keep key physiology markers in a healthy range. Those markers include blood pressure, body temperature, blood sugar, and energy balance.

When we experience stress, the brain interprets the situation as a threat. In response, it adjusts these physiology markers to put our body in a survival mode. This process, allostasis, attempts to bring these markers back into balance (homeostasis) after the stressor is gone.

This adaptive response serves much like ballast in a boat that keeps it steady in turbulent waters. Allostasis does the same for our bodies and brains when we face real or perceived stress. It plays a significant role in resiliency.[15]

Homeostasis and allostasis showcase how God marvelously created our bodies. King David described this marvel in Psalm 139:14. "I praise you because I am fearfully and wonderfully made; your works are wonderful, I know that full well." These systems testify to God's provision for everything we need to thrive.

However, chronic stress keeps these crucial markers outside their healthy range. If they remain unbalanced beyond a few days, the body experiences allostatic load, a term for wear and tear on our bodies.[16] Our load gets pushed to its limit, which hurts us. This overload can harm our bodies (e.g., decreased immunity) and our emotions (e.g., unremitting anxiety). It can undermine our relationships (e.g., withdrawal) and even erode our spiritual lives.

Allostatic load causes wear and tear to the human body and its systems and may come from one of several sources: repeated hits from several stressors, lack of the body's adaption to stress, prolonged response because of a delay in shutting down after a stressor is gone, and an inadequate response to stress.[17] The writer of Proverbs described this effect in Proverbs 14:30: "A heart at peace gives life to the body, but envy rots the bones."

## The Three Primary Sources of Stress

Chronic stress comes from three primary sources: interpersonal (our relationships), intrapersonal (our inner world of thoughts and feelings), and institutional (our work, the environment in which we live, or even our church). All three contributors overlap somewhat. It's helpful for us to discover which source most fuels our chronic stress. I've described those sources below.

### INTERPERSONAL

Interpersonal issues such as a strained marriage, a chronically sick child, or a rebellious teen can cause stress. Criticism from others,[18] early life stressors,[19] and relationship trauma can also contribute.[20]

Although my wife and I continue to prioritize a strong marriage with forty-four years of marriage behind us, two of our children created significant stress. Doctors diagnosed our youngest daughter with a brain tumor at age one. For twenty-five years we fought to save her life, which included ten brain surgeries, experimental treatment, financial strain, and extended travel to find the best care for her. She is thriving now (the tumor is gone), but for years we faced intense stress, not knowing what the latest MRI might reveal.

Concurrently, our oldest daughter almost transformed overnight from a perfect church kid to a rebellious teen. After years of therapy, residential-treatment camps, worry, and handwringing, she is doing well. Our relationship with her is strong. During those rebellious years, however, we experienced a double dose of stress from our daughters.

In a later chapter you'll see how one practice, Safeguard Safety, can specifically develop resilience to interpersonal stress.

### INTRAPERSONAL

Intrapersonal stress involves our emotions and our thinking. Relational conflict, work dissatisfaction, and spiritual dryness may fuel this stress. It often diminishes clear thinking if we don't apply resilience tools. Our minds can wander without our conscious awareness, which leads to worry about the future and/or rumination over the past.

Research has discovered that mind wandering fuels unhappiness. In one study, researchers used a smartphone app to pose questions to the participants in real time. After they examined thousands of responses, they drew three conclusions. First, our minds wander almost 50 percent of the time. Second, when they wander, we are less happy. Third, what we think about more accurately predicts our happiness than what we are doing. They concluded that a wandering mind is often an unhappy one.[21] The practice Audit Your Thoughts can become a powerful tool for you to resist this tendency.

Research shows that introverts struggle more with intrapersonal stress than do extroverts.[22] Genetics makes the difference. Introverts ruminate, worry, and experience anxiety more often than do extroverts. The negative effects from stress come not from the actual stress events themselves, but from how people perceive the events and what they tell themselves. Introverts yield to this tendency more often than extroverts.

Take heart, though, if you're an introvert.

Researchers counter with, "It is . . . important to remember that personality traits are not set like plaster but are malleable, with a wealth of evidence that traits change across the life span. . . . It would therefore be inappropriate to interpret the strong relation between personality and well-being as indicative of the immutability of human happiness."[23]

If you are an introvert like me, encourage yourself with this. Research show that genetic influences on stress resilience range from 30 to 60 percent, with the average being 50 percent.[24] Life experience over which we have no control counts for another 10 percent of stress resilience. That leaves an encouraging 40 percent we can attribute to the choices we make. This gives us a significant margin of opportunity to develop the practices.[25] Some studies even show that up to 70 percent of personality traits, including optimism, are dependent on how we respond to our environment.[26] In other words, we have choices that help grow our resilience.

## INSTITUTIONAL

Our work or even our church world can contribute significant stress.[27] When our jobs don't provide clear roles or meaningful work, stress results. Minimal job control, overwork, boredom, taking work home, a toxic environment, unpleasant bosses, and having no friends at work also contribute to institutional stress.

A stressful work environment can cause anhedonia,[28] a term to describe when we no longer feel pleasure from the activities we once enjoyed. Acute stress in the workplace, such as a reasonable project deadline, can increase our motivation at work. However chronic stress, such as a boss who is never satisfied, can diminish our motivation and our work enjoyment.

Researchers tell us that such stress affects our brain's reward circuits[29] and make us more dissatisfied with our jobs. Chronic stress can affect almost everything about us, from our relationships to our emotions to our spiritual lives.[30] The section below describes what chronic stress does. I've included a simple stress self-evaluation at the end of this chapter so you can evaluate your current stress level.

## The Effects of Stress

Because God designed our bodies with interconnected systems, when stress affects one system, it often affects the other systems. These systems include the immune system, cardiovascular system, metabolic system, and central nervous system. We more easily get sick because our immune system gets compromised. Our blood pressure rises, which can cause heart problems. Because stress both dampens the hormone leptin, which tells us we are full, and increases the hormone ghrelin, which makes us hungry, we can eat too much, which can lead to obesity and diabetes.

Stress inhibits healthy brain function. It can lead to mental struggles like depression, anxiety, and memory problems.[31] Brain cells in our memory center may atrophy.[32] Stress impairs these executive functions directed by the pre-frontal cortex:[33] attention, planning, problem-solving, and emotional self-control.[34]

Neuro-ophthalmologist and author Dr. Mithu Storoni notes the negative cognitive and physical effects from stress. "Seven areas of malfunction [are] likely to be experienced by anyone who is chronically stressed: weak control over attention [reduced emotional self-regulation], too much or too little cortisol [the stress hormone], altered synaptic plasticity [the brain becomes less malleable], an out-of-tune body clock [hinders good sleep], inflammation [weakens immunity], insulin resistance [can cause diabetes], and flagging motivation [affects work performance]."[35]

Chronic stress can even cause foggy brain, when you can't think clearly.[36] Even perceived stress can shrink the thinking centers of our brain.[37] Stress also harms our gastrointestinal system and can cause IBS (irritable bowel syndrome), acid reflux, and stomach ulcers.

One researcher made this sobering statement: "Stress-related disorders in the broadest sense . . . contribute more to the total all-cause morbidity burden than does cardiovascular disease."[38] That means that stress-related disorders kill more people than heart disease does.

Chronic stress also affects leadership in both a ministry and business context. It impairs decision-making and may incite aggressive behavior. Problem-solving gets compromised. It results in self-focus and leadership anxiety because it depletes our inner resources.[39] If you don't respond to stress with resilience, you can even become a source of stress to your reports and your supervisors.

Stress aggravates negative emotions like fear, anger, and worry because it enhances the growth of the amygdala, the brain part involved in these emotions. The amygdala gets stuck on high alert, which creates a shorter fuse. Defensiveness results, which can strain a relationship even if that relationship didn't cause the stress. Stress also compromises listening skills and empathy, both of which are crucial for healthy relationships.

Stress can even affect our walk with God. We lose perspective and blame God for our problems. We don't trust Him as we once did and may even relate to Him at arm's length, much like Jonah when his poor decisions brought him significant stress.

Ultimately, chronic stress can lead to burnout. When we understand burnout, it becomes a key insight upon which to build resilience and apply the nine practices.

## STRESS AND BURNOUT

Psychologist Christina Maslach[40] pioneered burnout research. She defines burnout as "a prolonged response to chronic emotional and interpersonal stressors on the job, and is defined by the three dimensions of exhaustion, cynicism, and inefficacy."[41] She visualizes it with this metaphor: "The word [burnout] evokes images of a final flickering flame, of a charred and empty shell, of dying embers and cold, gray ashes."[42]

She created the most widely used burnout inventory, the Maslach Burnout Inventory, which you can purchase to evaluate your burnout level. Although she applies burnout to the workplace, burnout can occur regardless of your job status.

Burnout begins with emotional exhaustion when you feel overextended and depleted, with nothing left to give. Spiritual dryness plays a role in emotional exhaustion.[43] Emotional exhaustion affects relationships, which leads to the second stage, depersonalization, when we detach ourselves from others. This leads to the third stage, reduced accomplishment. You feel incompetent or unproductive.[44]

Author and researcher Anne-Laure Le Cunff renames exhaustion, depersonalization, and inefficacy with weariness, withdrawal, and worry.[45]

Weariness happens when we lack the emotional energy to do our job, and we may overwork. Withdrawal occurs when we lose our passion for the work and pull away from others, even those outside of the work environment.

Finally, we worry when we doubt our ability to do the job correctly. We may lack confidence to do it or our bosses may seldom recognize us for a job well done. A corollary to burnout, "bore-out," describes what happens when our jobs chronically bore us from sameness or lack of challenge.[46] Bore-out can create the same negative effects as burnout.

Unless we deal with burnout, it can start a destructive chronic stress loop that feeds on itself. We make poor decisions that lead to an unhealthy lifestyle. We overeat, overspend, isolate ourselves from others, or even abuse drugs and alcohol. These choices then lead to more chronic illness, which reinforces prior chronic stress, a never-ending feedback loop illustrated below.

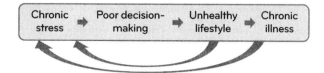

| Chronic stress | → | Poor decision-making | → | Unhealthy lifestyle | → | Chronic illness |

However, when we build resilience with the nine practices, we can transform these three burnout components into positive qualities. Resilience can turn exhaustion into engagement with our work. It can transform depersonalization into renewed involvement with others. It can change inefficacy into efficacy, when we feel empowered and believe that we can the job well. If we struggle with burnout (or bore-out), the practices will give us tools to develop resilience and deepen your relationship with Jesus (John 10:10).

We've seen that chronic stress is a "big bad wolf." As you consider your level of chronic stress, take this short quiz below. The more "yes" answers you select, that the more stress could be an issue for you. You made a good choice to read this book.

In the next chapter we'll explore resilience. I'll define and illustrate it. You'll learn its positive benefits. And you'll also take away a framework for the nine practices that follow in the later chapters.

## Chronic Stress Inventory

Answer these ten questions about the effects from chronic stress. The more you answer yes, the more you may need to prioritize your Stress Resilience Plan.

1. I often feel that life is overwhelming. __yes __no

2. I get irritable more often without cause. __yes __no

3. I rarely sleep well. __yes __no

4. I'm losing interest in what I once enjoyed and find little to be grateful for. __yes __no

5. I often feel spiritually dry. __yes __no

6. I more often get sick and recover more slowly. __yes __no

7. I often feel sad, fearful, and/or depressed. __yes __no

8. I can't concentrate and pay attention as well as I once could. __yes __no

9. I feel pulled to withdraw from others. __yes __no

10. I'm eating junk food too often, exercising less, watching too much TV, and/or using too much alcohol. __yes __no

## APPLICATION

1. What did the inventory reveal to you?

2. From which of the three stress sources does most of your stress arise: interpersonal (our relationships), intrapersonal (our inner world of thoughts and feelings), or institutional (our environment and our work)? How could you lower your stress in that area?

3. What is the biggest contributing factor in the source you chose in the prior question? Why do you think that is so?

4. What do you hope this book might offer to increase your stress resilience?

For downloadable tools, visit this web link: www.charlesstone.com/stress.

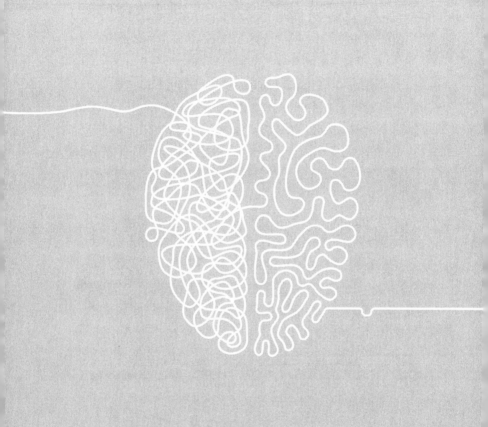

# 3

# What Resilience Is
# and What It Does

*The oak fought the wind and was broken,
the willow bent when it must and survived.*

**ROBERT JORDAN**

*(1948–2007)*

magine that you registered for a seminar on resilience offered by your
local junior college. You arrive early to get a good seat. You notice three
coffee tables onstage, all with glass tops. The seminar starts, and the speaker
introduces himself. He then asks the audience to imagine what would
happen to each table given three scenarios.

In one scenario, he holds a heavy rock six feet above one table.

He asks the audience, "What would happen if I dropped the rock on
the glass?" Several people shout, "The glass would shatter!"

Holding an egg over the second table, he next asks, "What would
happen if I dropped the egg on the glass?" Everyone chuckles and someone
yells, "The egg will crack and make a mess."

He then moves to the third table with a tennis ball in hand and asks,
"What would happen if I dropped the ball on the glass?" Observers respond with, "The ball would bounce and the glass wouldn't break."

Then, for dramatic effect, he stands behind the first table and actually drops the rock, but grabs it just before it hits the glass top. He reminds the people that sending shards into the audience would not help with new speaking engagements.

He moves to the second table, drops the egg, and it bursts open, leaving a gooey mess on the glass.

He shifts over to the third table and drops the tennis ball. As expected, it bounces without damaging the glass or making a mess.

By now, the speaker has gained your attention.

He says, "Folks, this experiment illustrates resilience." The rock represents people with no resilience. When under stress, they break stuff: relationships, teamwork, even their own health. The egg also represents people with no resilience. When they experience stress, they crack up and make messes of their own lives and often others' lives as well.

However, the tennis ball illustrates a resilient person. Although the tennis ball faced the same "circumstance" as the rock and the egg (resistance from the glass), it responded differently. Resilient people face similar resistance to their lives, their goals, and their relationships as do non-resilient people. The resilient ones, however, flex, bend, and bounce back.

This imagined scenario visually illustrates resilience. The short definition for resilience is *the ability to bounce back from life's stressful circumstances*. Resilience comes from the Latin word *resalire*, which means to bounce back or jump again. The egg represents a lack of resilience: too much give, while the rock also represents a lack of resilience: no give. Researchers have discovered that resilience measures how well we cope with stress.[1] It helps keep our bodies and brains in a homeostatic balance to avoid allostatic load, the wear and tear stress places on us. Stress resilience is our goal and the nine practices are the means.

Many researchers have discovered how resilience helps us manage stress. Daniel Goleman, most known for his work on emotional intelligence, writes, "More than education, more than experience, more than training, a person's level of resilience will determine who succeeds and who fails. That's true in the cancer ward, it's true in the Olympics, and it's true in the boardroom."[2] Although Goleman may have overstated things a bit, his quote reinforces our need to develop resilience. Mayo Clinic researchers examined almost two thousand executives in an executive health clinic and found a significant relationship between resilience and coping with stress and well-being.[3]

However, resilience differs from stress management and simply coping. One researcher emphasized this when he wrote, "Resilience is more than bouncing back from adversity. People who are resilient keep pursuing their goals in the face of challenges. Consequently, learning how to regulate your brain's motivational machinery is a key aspect of resilience."[4]

Stress management means that we have coped with a stressful situation. It involves a look back at the situation, like looking into the rearview mirror when we drive. Resilience, however, looks forward to potential stress, like looking through a car's windshield. Successful driving requires that we spend more time looking forward through the windshield than looking back into the rearview mirror. Likewise, resilience also requires a forward look to prepare us to better respond to our next stressor. For example, when you recover from unfair criticism from your boss or spouse, you have managed your stress (the rearview look). When you learn from it to become better prepared for future criticisms (the forward look), you have grown your resilience.[5]

So resilience involves much more than bouncing back or coping. Dr. Amit Sood, one of the world's leaders on resilience, defines it in this way: "Resilience is your ability to withstand adversity (resist), bounce back from adversity (recover), and grow despite life's downturns (rise)."[6]

The American Psychological Association defines it as "the process of adapting well in the face of adversity, trauma, tragedy, threats and even significant sources of stress—such as family and relationship problems, serious health problems, or workplace and financial stresses."[7]

University psychologist George Vaillant describes a resilient person as being like "a twig with a fresh, green living core. When twisted out of shape, such a twig bends, but it does not break; instead, it springs back and continues growing."[8]

## The Bible on Resilience to Stress

Resilience relates to the concept of human flourishing, a phrase that would describe an aspect of the abundant life Jesus offers (John 10:10). Jesus wants us to flourish in this life. Although He doesn't promise problem-free living, we're not selfish when we desire to grow our resilience so that we flourish even more. However, we must root this desire in biblical truth.

Dr. Jonathan Pennington, mentioned earlier, writes this about human flourishing:

> [It] is a key biblical theme woven through the entire canon, one which explains and enhances some foundational aspects of the Bible's testimony, including the very nature and goal of God's redemption for us in Christ, who promises us eternal and abundant life. That is, the Bible, across its whole Christian canon of both Old and New Testaments, provides its own God-of-Israel-revealed-in-Jesus-Christ answer to the foundational human question of how to flourish and thrive.[9]

Pennington also notes three clusters of biblical ideas that relate to human flourishing.

The first is *shālôm/eirēnē/peace*. This cluster points to the idea of wholeness that results in well-being as God's people rightly relate to Him and others.

The second cluster is *'ashrê /makarios/blessedness/happiness*. We flourish, experience happiness, only through a relationship with God.

The final cluster is *tāmîm/teleios/wholeness*. This cluster overlaps with shalom.

He notes,

> Whereas *shālôm* and *'ashrê* largely function as descriptors of human flourishing from an overview perspective, *tāmîm* describes the means by which and that state wherein a human can experience God-directed and God-blessed flourishing, through wholeness.

> As one pursues this wholeness of heart, one experiences human flourishing and well-being, not only because this is natural as God has ordered the world, but also because this way of being in the world accords with God's reign and thereby brings *shālôm* and *'ashrê*.[10]

Scripture describes many biblical characters who faced stress. Their experiences remind us that in this life we will face suffering (Matt. 5:10; 2 Tim. 3:12; 1 Peter 3:14). Yet, as we keep Christ central to our lives through faith and practicing spiritual disciplines (including resilience skills), it need not defeat us.

The apostle Paul experienced chronic stress most of his Christian life, yet showed resilience in almost every situation. Examples include angry mobs (Acts 13:50), being stoned and left for dead (Acts 14:19), beaten and imprisoned (Acts 16:16–24), and shipwrecked (Acts 27:39–44). He captures his life of chronic stress in 2 Corinthians 11:23–28:

> I have worked much harder, been in prison more frequently, been flogged more severely, and been exposed to death again and again. Five times I received from the Jews the forty lashes minus one. Three times I was beaten with rods, once I was pelted with stones, three times I was shipwrecked, I spent a night and a day in the open sea, I have been constantly on the move. I have been in danger from rivers, in danger from bandits, in danger from my fellow Jews, in danger from Gentiles; in danger in the city, in danger in the country, in danger at sea; and in

danger from false believers. I have labored and toiled and have often gone without sleep; I have known hunger and thirst and have often gone without food; I have been cold and naked. Besides everything else, I face daily the pressure of my concern for all the churches.

At one point, he even wrote that he despaired of life itself (2 Cor. 1:8). Other places he recorded severe trials (2 Cor. 8:2), troubles, hardships, distresses (2 Cor. 6:4), and suffering (Phil. 1:29). He saw these stressful experiences as tools in God's hand to strengthen him. He wrote, "For Christ's sake, I delight in weaknesses, in insults, in hardships, in persecutions, in difficulties. For when I am weak, then I am strong" (2 Cor. 12:10).

In 2 Corinthians 4:8–9, he detailed how resilience benefits us. "We are hard pressed on every side, but not crushed; perplexed, but not in despair; persecuted, but not abandoned; struck down, but not destroyed." He follows each stressful description with the word "but," which transitions to his resilient responses: not crushed, not in despair, not abandoned, and not destroyed. Paul consistently showed resilience in the face of stress because he kept these practices. He focused on his identity in Christ (2 Cor. 5:17), kept a healthy perspective on difficulty (1 Cor. 4:7–10), and metacognitively focused his thoughts on the Lord (Col. 3:1–2) and on that which was good (Phil. 4:8). Metacognition means to think about your thinking.

Paul understood the power of Christ to build resilience and grow character. He wrote, "And we boast in the hope of the glory of God. Not only so, but we also glory in our sufferings, because we know that suffering produces perseverance; perseverance, character; and character, hope. And hope does not put us to shame, because God's love has been poured out into our hearts through the Holy Spirit, who has been given to us" (Rom. 5:2–5).

# Key Resilience Concepts

The concepts below will help you understand and apply the practices in the following chapters.

## NATURE AND NURTURE TOGETHER DETERMINE RESILIENCE

Resilience comes easier for some people because their genetic makeup predisposes them toward resilience. "Bouncing back is a choice—but the choice is easier for some."[11] Some studies show that we have a happiness set-point that we can change by increasing our resilience.[12] Skills like these resilience practices can boost your resilience set-point.[13]

## MULTIPLE FACTORS INFLUENCE RESILIENCE

Research shows several factors impact resilience.[14] Factors include the following, and the practices detail what they are and how to apply them.

- realistic optimism
- facing fear with courage
- planning and problem-solving
- a strong moral compass and strong values
- faith
- social support and resilient role models
- physical fitness
- brain fitness
- cognitive reappraisal and positive reframing
- positive emotions and emotional flexibility
- meaning, purpose, and accomplishment
- tenacity

## RESILIENCE FACTORS ARE ADDITIVE

Neuroscientists Dr. Golnaz Tabibnia and Dr. Dan Redecki[15] note that certain skills and strategies (see the above list) can rewire our brains to boost resilience. These skills and strategies are additive. "Having and strengthening multiple resilience-building skills will increase the likelihood of resilience."[16]

The more you develop and practice resilience skills, the more likely you will respond well to stress. As you develop your Stress Resilience Growth Plan (template available for download at www.charlesstone .com/stress), you'll add many skills you can adapt to specific stressful situations.

## RESILIENCE IS NOT BINARY

A complete view of stress covers a continuum from distress to eustress (good stress). Resilience also exists on a continuum with many factors at play. It's not that either you have it or you don't. Resilience incorporates learned skills and beliefs that change.[17]

Researchers Debra Nelson and Bret Simmons apply the analogy of taking a tub bath when they write, "A more complete model of stress [and resilience] should acknowledge that there are two faucets (hot and cold) and that managing both are necessary if you want to get the water level and temperature just right for a comfortable bath. Few individuals take a totally cold bath (distress) or a totally hot bath (eustress). Similarly, few, if any stressors, are appraised as purely positive or purely negative. It is usually some combination of the two."[18] Resilience is much the same.

## RESILIENCE INCLUDES THREE CORE COMPONENTS

Resilience theories overlap in three ways. A resilient person will show all three.[19] First, resilient people accept reality as it is. Second, they make meaning out of difficulty, as did Victor Frankl, a psychiatrist who survived the Nazi death camps. He wrote in his book *Man's Search for Meaning,* "We must never forget that we may also find meaning in life even when confronted with a hopeless situation, when facing a fate that cannot be changed."[20] Finally, they make do with what is at hand by improvising, being flexible in the moment.

## RESILIENCE IS BOTH A STATE AND A TRAIT

A resilient person will respond well in a stressful moment (a *state* response) and will respond well long-term (a *trait* response). This relates to the rearview mirror/windshield illustration used earlier. We know our resilience is growing when we ingrain the practices more often into our day-to-day experience with stress.[21] The apostle Paul would call this character when he writes that suffering (stress) produces character (Rom. 5:4).

## RESILIENCE INCLUDES RECOVERY

Sometimes we view resilience as a slog through difficulty, going one more round, or gutting it out. Although sometimes we must respond in those ways, balanced resilience includes recovery from stress. "The key to resilience is trying really hard, then stopping, recovering, and then trying again. This conclusion is based on the biology of homeostasis. When the body is out of alignment from overworking [chronic stress that results in allostatic load], we waste [a lot of] mental and physical resources trying to return to balance before we can move forward."[22]

## MULTIPLE BRAIN NETWORKS INFLUENCE RESILIENCE

God designed our brains more like malleable putty than fixed porcelain. The term for this quality, neuroplasticity, refers to "the ability of the nervous system to respond to intrinsic or extrinsic stimuli by reorganizing its structure, function and connections."[23] Several networks play a role in our neuroplastic response to stress. They include the fear network, the reward network, and the default mode network, the network active when we daydream and aren't focusing on a specific task. Refer to the prior chapters for a more detailed view of the stress response.

One study examined stress that forty-eight medical students experienced during an internship.[24] They discovered a specific location in the brain (the noradrenergic locus coeruleus, NE-LC) that provided a marker for resilience. This brain part produces norepinephrine, the neurotransmitter involved in the stress response. When these students felt stressed, their NE-LC became more hyperactive. Greater activity showed a lack of resilience. Less activity showed greater adaptability and resilience. The practices you'll learn can keep this part of your brain calmer when in a stressful situation.

## How Resilience Benefits Us

Stress resilience benefits us in multiple ways. We bounce back from stress more quickly. Our work performance and relationships improve,[25] including our relationship with the Lord. It can help reduce anxiety and depression, which enhances health. It minimizes burnout. Well-being, flourishing, and joy increase. It enhances empathy. Problem-solving skills improve because you engage your brain's thinking centers so you know what to do in a stressful situation.

It increases the threshold for sparking the stress response. Resilience keeps the amygdala, our brain's fear switch, from switching on unnecessarily. It keeps our fear network from being too sensitive to avoid sending a hormonal "fire truck" to put out a stress fire when none exists. It regulates our fear response to bring it more in line with the degree a threat poses.[26]

Resilience can protect us from serious health issues like cancer, chronic pain, and addictions.[27] It can even reduce the degree that stress contributes to inflammation,[28] which lies at the source of many serious diseases. Resilience may even help us live longer, especially when we keep strong relationships.[29]

In this chapter, I visualized resilience with the rock, egg, tennis ball metaphor. Keep that metaphor in keep mind as you learn about the practices and build your Stress Resilience Growth Plan. I also shared several Scriptures about resilience. Consider memorizing one of them as you develop your plan. I concluded the chapter with key concepts and how resilience benefits us. In the next chapter, you'll begin to build your plan with Practice 1: Cease and Breathe. I have not listed the nine practices in order of importance. However, it's best to read them in the sequence listed to help you develop your growth plan.

### APPLICATION

1. Which part of the rock, egg, and tennis ball illustration do you most identify with? Why?

2. The chapter includes some Scriptures about the apostle Paul's experience with stress. Who else in the Bible faced stress? How did they deal with it?

3. Review the key resilience concepts. What do those concepts reveal about your current level of resilience? What might you change in the future to enhance your resilience?

4. Contrast where you'd currently evaluate yourself on the resilience continuum with a time in the past. How does your response to stress today differ from the past?

5. What is one verse you could memorize as you read this book?

For downloadable tools, visit this web link: www.charlesstone.com/stress.

PART 2

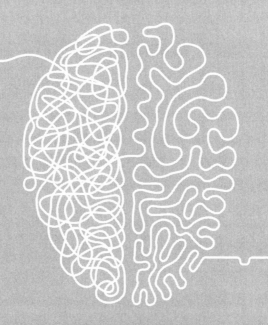

The
Practices

This section begins the first chapter to unpack the first of nine practices. Each chapter will include the biblical basis that supports the practice, the brain insight behind it, and the best practice(s) to apply to develop your stress resilience. The first four practices relate to "in the heat of the moment" use when you face an acute stress situation. I call these four "state" practices. The last five reflect habits that build a stress resilience lifestyle. I call them "trait" practices.

You'd apply a state practice when you feel acute stress and apply the trait practice as an ongoing way of life. But don't draw a hard line between the two. Your state practices will probably become a lifestyle, and you'll probably find the trait practices helpful in moments of intense stress as well. Biblical truth and brain science undergird them all.

Expect some practices to resonate more with you than others. That's okay. Try them all and master the few you believe could best help you develop stress resilience. The downloadable Stress Resilience Growth Plan available at www.charlesstone.com/stress will help you organize, recall, and apply the practices.

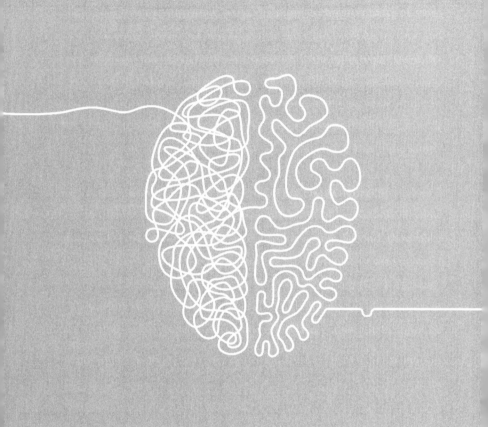

4

## PRACTICE 1:
# Cease and Breathe

*Conscious breathing heightens awareness
and deepens relaxation.*

**DAN BRULE**
*teacher/trainer*

*Let everything that has breath praise the LORD.*

**PSALM 150:6**

*Big idea:* Leverage your breath to enhance your resilience.

*Bible insight:* Both the Old and the New Testaments often refer to
our breath.

*Brain insight:* Slow, deep breathing activates a key nerve that calms
the brain's stress response.

*Best practice:* The STOPP resilience building skill.

The first practice, Cease and Breathe, summarizes this chapter's big idea:
In stressful moments, slow, deep breathing can calm your emotions.

To *cease and breathe* means to pause intentionally during a stressful
moment, pay attention to your breathing, slightly change its cadence, and

pray. Research has found that this activity calms your brain's stress circuits.[1] The acronym STOPP gives a simple way to recall and apply this practice. The letters stand for these steps.

> **S** stands for *Stop what you're doing.*
> **T** stands for *Take a breath.*
> **O** stands for *Observe your thoughts and emotions.*
> The first **P** stands for *Pray your Jesus Prayer* (more on the Jesus Prayer below).
> The second **P** stands for *Proceed.*

## What About the Breath?

Think for a moment about your breath.

Breathing is something we do without thinking. If you live into your seventies, you will have taken almost a billion breaths and the air you have breathed would weigh almost three hundred tons.[2] God hardwired our brains to make our lungs breathe without our conscious thought. Yet we can also consciously control our breathing.

Divers take a deep breath to steady themselves, focus, and send the maximum oxygen to their brains before they jump off the diving board. When we try to thread the eye of a needle, we often hold our breath to steady our hands. Parents who attend birthing classes learn to breathe rhythmically together during childbirth to lessen the mom's pain. Breathing provides a good barometer of our current emotional and mental state. It's always with us. So, what do the Scriptures say about our breath?

## Biblical Insight on the Breath

The Bible mentions the breath more than seventy-five times. The common Hebrew word for breath is *ruach,* first used in Genesis in the creation account when God "breathed into his [Adam's] nostrils the breath of life, and the man became a living being" (Gen. 2:7). *Ruach* can mean breath, wind, or spirit. The writer of Genesis reminds us that God animated the first human beings with His breath. God's breath served as a unique symbol and sign of humanity, distinguishing us from the rest of creation.

Job, the Old Testament patriarch, realized that God's breath gave him life and spiritual vitality. "The Spirit of God has made me; the breath of the Almighty gives me life" (Job 33:4). The psalmist reflects a similar idea in Psalm 104:29–30, "When you hide your face, they are terrified; when you take away their breath, they die and return to the dust. When you send your Spirit, they are created, and you renew the face of the ground."

After the great prophet Elijah won a powerful spiritual victory over the pagan prophets of Baal, he hid in a cave to escape execution by the pagan king's wife Jezebel. While in the cave he heard "the sound of a soft breath" (1 Kings 19:12 BBE), the breath or whisper of God. A prophecy meant to give hope to Israel describes how God animated a valley of dry bones with His breath (Ezek. 37).

The ancient Jews practiced a prayer when they inhaled and exhaled on every letter of the Hebrew word for God, YHWH. They breathed the word for the name of God rather than speaking the word because they believed that God's name was unspeakable. Of course believers aren't bound by that practice; we have the privilege of reverently speaking God's name.

The New Testament also uses the word *breath*. The Greek word for breath, *pneuma*, correlates to the Hebrew word *ruach*. After Jesus rose from the dead and first appeared to His disciples, He gave them the gift of the Holy Spirit. The book of Acts describes this act as breathing. "And with that he breathed on them and said, 'Receive the Holy Spirit'" (John 20:22). Just as God breathed physical life into Adam, Jesus breathed spiritual life into the early church to give them and us spiritual life. Even the English word *spiritual* reflects the breath. It comes from the Latin word *spiritualis,* which means *of breathing.*

## Brain Insight on the Breath

God created our bodies so that we breathe automatically. He designed our biology so that our breathing could also counter stress. Deep breathing stimulates one of the twelve pairs of cranial nerves, nerves that don't first pass through the spinal cord. These nerves connect our brain to other parts of the body through electrical signals. One key nerve pair, called the vagal (or vagus) nerve, weaves through our hollow organs like the heart, lungs, and stomach. It got its name from the word *vagrant*. Just as vagrants wander from place to place, the vagal nerve wanders about our hollow organs, which provides a strong connection to our brain. Since in one way we experience stress in our hollow organs, this nerve performs a critical role in stress resilience.

Stress evokes certain sensations in these hollow organs. We may get butterflies, our stomach may churn, we may feel our heart rate increase, anxious feelings may rise from deep within, etc. These normal bodily responses occur when we face threat, danger, or uncertainty. However, a perpetually engaged stress system harms our bodies and brains. Stress can dampen the vagal nerve's calming effects. But when we intentionally engage the vagal nerve through slow deep breathing, those uncomfortable body sensations can diminish. Deep breathing engages the vagal nerve, as neuroscientist Dr. Alex Korb explains:

> Breathing affects the brain through signals carried by the vagus nerve. Not only does the vagus nerve send signals down to the heart . . . , but it also carries signals up into the brain stem. Vagus nerve signaling is important in activating circuits for resting and relaxation, known as the parasympathetic nervous system. The parasympathetic system is the opposite of the sympathetic nervous system, which controls the fight-or-flight instinct. Slow breathing increases activity in the vagus nerve and pushes the brain toward parasympathetic activity. So slow, deep breathing calms you down.[3]

When this nerve gets engaged, it activates our brain's emotional brake, the parasympathetic nervous system. This reduces the stress response, decreases the stress hormone cortisol, and increases attention.[4] Deep breathing, especially the out breath, engages this important nerve.[5]

## Best Practice: STOPP

Every day when we drive, we see a common sight: stop signs. When we see one, we stop, or should stop. If we don't stop, we risk getting a ticket, or worse, we might cause an accident. The stop sign image can help you remember and apply this practice. STOPP stands for these simple steps to do when in a stressful moment, and it expands upon the STOP skill widely used in mindfulness training.[6] I've included these once again to help you remember them.

Stop what you are doing.

Take a breath.

Observe what's going on within you and without.

Pray.

Proceed with your day.

This skill not only helps us deal with stress as it comes, but prepares us to handle it before it comes. It helps us take mini-moments during the day to disengage from our current stressful tasks. The ancient monastics practiced this. They called it *statio,* which means "station" or "position" in Latin. It served as a physical and spiritual pause between tasks to prepare mentally for the next task.[7]

*Statio* became a daily discipline that cultivated God's presence in the mundane tasks of life. More than a physical pause, it became a holy pause that acknowledged God's presence and a reminder to not hurry. Author-philosopher Dallas Willard said that we must "ruthlessly eliminate hurry" from our lives to grow spiritually.[8] This practice cultivates awareness about our next task and can keep us from mindlessly forging ahead with it. It helps us become more present in the moment.

Those who arranged the Psalms describe a similar pause with the word *selah* that appears seventy-one times in the Psalms, at the middle or the end of a verse. It invited the gathered community to pause for private reflection on that psalm's theme.[9]

In summary, *statio* is a moment between moments when we pause from one task before going to the next. It allows us to break our hurry, focus on the Lord, respond to stress, get closure from the prior task, and prepare our hearts and minds for what comes next.

We practice *statio* as we apply the STOPP skill. As we do, we can turn down our body's stress accelerator and engage our body's stress brake (the vagal nerve) to experience greater calm.

Let's unpack each component. Realize that this skill may take you thirty seconds or a few minutes to apply, depending upon the severity of the acute stress event in your unique circumstance.

**S** simply means to stop your current activity. When you feel stress rising or you experience an acute stress situation (e.g., you had an argument with your spouse or child), simply stop what you are doing. You might need to move to a different room or pull over for a moment if you're in your car. You may need to separate yourself from another person for a few minutes. A walk may help. This first step begins the calming process.

**T** means to take a breath. Remember, God designed deep breathing to disengage our stress response by enervating the vagal nerve. So, after you have stopped your activity, take a few slow, deep breaths. You might experiment with these different breathing techniques to find the one that works best for you. The 4-7-8 breathing technique involves slowly inhaling for a count of four, holding your breath for a count of seven, and then exhaling for a count of eight.[10] Another breathing technique, box breathing that is used by the Navy Seals,[11] involves breathing in four seconds, holding your breath for four seconds, breathing out for four seconds, and then holding your breath for four seconds. Whatever technique works for you, use it to take three or four breaths.

**O** stands for observe. After you've calmed yourself a bit with deep breathing, take a third person's perspective to notice your inner and outer world. Ask yourself a few questions like these:

- What circumstance is causing me to feel stressed?
- Is this circumstance causing me stress, or is it tapping into a prior experience?
- How am I interpreting this circumstance?
- What story am I telling myself about this situation?
- Does what I am telling myself jibe with reality or with biblical truth?
- Do I feel threatened, uncertain, or fearful?
- What physical sensations do I feel in my body?
- What emotions do I feel?

Your goal is not to change your circumstance, although you may need to get out of harm's way. Nor is it to force your unpleasant emotions to vanish or to ignore them. Rather, to observe means to notice dispassionately and describe the stress-evoking situation and what you are feeling and thinking in the circumstance. Practice 4 will explain this idea in more depth. It's called metacognition,[12] thinking about your thinking.[13] It's the ability to step back and think about your thoughts and your own mental state, to observe, and be aware of your thinking.

**P** stands for pray.

Breathing to deal with stress predates neuroscience. The ancient monastic Christians practiced a meditation that incorporated breathing with prayer. They understood how our minds chatter and distract us from spiritual focus, a consequence of stress. They also understood how our minds drift and wander from thinking about God or Scripture. One ancient Christian wrote, "Let the name of Jesus adhere to your breath, and then you will know the blessings of stillness."[14] This monastic noticed he could quiet his thoughts when he paired breathing with prayer. By giving his mind something to do, focus on a biblical phrase while coupling it to awareness of the breath itself, he could calm his mind. It's something akin to a mental piece of red string tied around your finger to jog your mind when it drifts.

Monastics would prescribe various Scripture verses and prayers as antidotes to different distracting thoughts and use these opportunities to immerse themselves in Scripture and prayer. This prayer became a common one. They called it the Jesus Prayer. It combined Luke 18:39, "Son of David, have mercy on me!" with Luke 18:13, "God, have mercy on me, a sinner." As they breathed in, they would silently pray, "Jesus, Son of David." As they breathed out, they would pray silently, "Have mercy on me, a sinner." The Jesus Prayer concept applies to the first P in the STOPP skill. Studies show that such prayer reduces stress.[15]

Thus far you have paused your activity at the moment, taken a few deep breaths, and observed what is happening inside you and in your external circumstances. Now combine a prayer with breathing, something like the Jesus Prayer.

You don't have to use the exact phrase the ancients used. Choose your own. A common prayer you often pray might work. It might be a combination of a portion of Bible verses meaningful to you. A simple memorized prayer could fit. A prayer that matches the current stress circumstance you're facing may work.

Let's assume you got some bad news from a medical test. Your version of the Jesus Prayer for that stress situation might go something like this. As you breathe in, you pray, "Lord Jesus, You are the great physician." You pause briefly as you hold your breath a bit. Then as you breathe out you might pray, "I have feelings of fear, but I trust You." Whatever prayer you feel most comfortable with, repeat it several times. Remember, the Bible often speaks about the breath and about prayer, and brain insight tells us how breathing can diminish the stress response.

Of course, you don't want to turn these prayers into rote mechanical repetitions. Jesus cautions us against that in Matthew 6:7. Remind yourself that the purpose behind the Jesus Prayer in a stressful situation is to shift your thoughts to God as you turn down the brain's stress response through your breathing.

The final **P** means proceed with your day. The STOPP skill may only take thirty seconds. Or it may take a few minutes, depending on the circumstance. I've created a downloadable tool (www.charlesstone.com/stress) that visualizes this skill. Print it out and place in a place you'll see it often, like your car's dashboard or your bathroom mirror.

## REVIEW

*Big idea:* Leverage your breath to enhance your resilience.

*Bible insight:* Both the Old and the New Testaments often refer to the breath.

*Brain insight:* Slow breathing activates a key nerve that calms the brain's stress response.

*Best practice:* The STOPP resilience building skill.

## APPLICATION

1. Write down one to three key ideas from this chapter.

2. What visual or electronic prompts can you create to remind yourself to apply the STOPP skill when you face a stressful situation?

3. Practice the STOPP skill each day for a week. Afterward, debrief the experience. How did it go? How did you feel afterward? What you might you do differently next time you apply the skill?

Download the Stress Resilience Plan here and follow directions to begin to fill it out: www.charlesstone.com/stress.

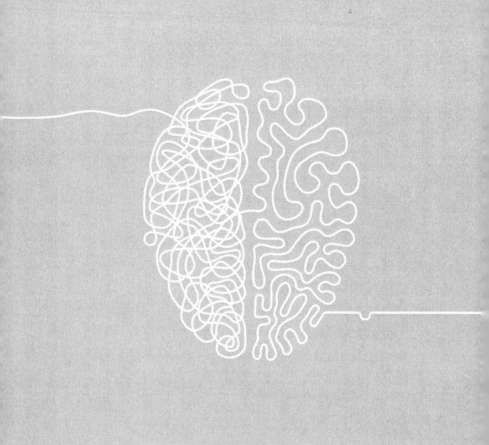

5

PRACTICE 2:

# Reveal How You Feel

*Emotions are indicators, not dictators.*
*They can indicate where your heart is in the moment,*
*but that doesn't mean they have the right*
*to dictate your behavior.*

**LYSA TERKEURST**
*author*

*Big idea:* Resolve unpleasant emotions before chronic stress develops.

*Bible insight:* Scripture illustrates how several biblical characters handled their emotions. Some did well. Some didn't.

*Brain insight:* When you name an unpleasant emotion (called affect labeling), you down-regulate its intensity.

*Best practice:* Notice, Name, and Distance.

'm an expert at Whac-a-Mole, a game you'll find in many arcades.

I honed my expert skills years ago when I took our kids to the arcade each summer we vacationed in Myrtle Beach. The game console includes a soft hammer attached to a board with several cup-sized holes in it. When you drop a quarter into the slot and the game begins, moles randomly pop up and down in the holes. The goal is to whack the moles back into the holes before they drop back in themselves. The more moles you whack, the better your score, and the more prize tickets spit out from the front of the game console. I recall one prize I got when I redeemed my tickets, a tiny green toy soldier with a plastic parachute. I think I still own it. In case you're wondering, I gave most of my tickets to my kids.

Whac-a-Mole pictures how we sometimes try to whack away unpleasant emotions like fear, depression, or anxiety. We whack them when we misapply a spiritual discipline. We whack them when we stuff, ignore, or deny them. Some whack them by overeating, overspending, or abusing drugs and alcohol.

The only problem with the Whac-a-Mole method—which I've often used—is that it seldom works. I've wrongly assumed that the right spiritual disciplines practiced in the right order in the right way would yield the exact results I wanted. I assumed God would take away my unpleasant emotion. I viewed God as a celestial vending machine; push the right spiritual buttons and He'd remove the emotion.

Over the years I've more wisely responded to these stress-induced emotions as I've learned how they work. Our emotions include both a spiritual and a body/brain/biological component. Neuroscientists have discovered that when we use the Whac-a-Mole method, we strengthen those very emotions we try to erase.[1] They rebound with greater power. When stress creates unpleasant emotions like anxiety, fear, and worry, we might deal with them in different ways. Prayer and Bible reading might suffice. We might need counseling. Medicine might be appropriate in some situations. The tools I suggest below might work for you. Or a combination of these might work best.

Unpleasant emotions are not necessarily bad or sinful. Emotions play a significant role in defining us as human. They add color to life. Dr. Rhyne R. Putman, professor of theology and culture at New Orleans Baptist

Theological Seminary, notes these insights about emotions: "Scripture presents reason and emotion as inseparably linked gifts from God."[2] It does not "compartmentalize emotion and reason in its treatment of human decision-making and behavior. We feel around our world before we reason about it."[3]

He notes that the Hebrew term *lev*, most often translated "heart," describes personality in its entirety, our inner life and character. The related Greek term used in the Septuagint (the Greek version of the Hebrew Bible) and the New Testament, *kardia*, describes the "inseparable yet distinguishable relationship of reason, emotion, and volition."[4] The word describes the inner life as both the center of our personality and the place where the Holy Spirit evokes deep inner change.

Putman writes that emotions play a crucial role in our Christian experience. They don't produce genuine faith. Automatic intuitions don't determine our beliefs. Scripture, however, teaches us that "sin can distort our emotions and intuitions, and as a result, our beliefs. . . . The Christian believer must ultimately submit his or her emotions to the authority of Scripture and the lordship of Christ."[5]

Spiritual disciplines and confession don't always affect these unpleasant emotions, as the late Tim Keller noted,

> We must beware of giving people the impression that through individual repentance for sin they should be able to undo their personal problems [and feel better]. Obviously, we should not go to the other nonbiblical extreme of refusing to acknowledge personal responsibility for sinful behavior as well. . . . While we can't fall into the reductionism of believing all problems are chemically based and require medication, we also cannot fall into the reductionism of believing all problems [and difficult emotions] are simply a matter of lacking spiritual disciplines.[6]

This chapter covers the general topic of emotion regulation.[7] You'll learn what Scripture and science say about emotions. And you'll learn how to apply this chapter's practice, Reveal How You Feel, so you can further develop your stress resilience.

## Bible Insight on Emotions

The Bible reveals much about difficult emotions like worry, anxiety, depression, and anger. The apostle Paul implied he struggled with anxiety when he wrote about sending a fellow servant to the church in Philippi, "Therefore I am all the more eager to send him, so that when you see him again you may be glad and I may have less anxiety" (Phil. 2:28). The word *anxiety* means mental anguish, an unpleasant emotion Paul experienced.

He also wrote, "Do not be anxious about anything" (Phil. 4:6). This word for anxiety means to brood, ruminate, or excessively repeat some worrisome thought in our minds. It's like a movie on a DVD that gets stuck and repeats the same scene over and over. Only this time the scene reflects a real or imagined experience in our minds that intensifies unpleasant emotions. The more we replay the scene through negative, critical, or judgmental chatter, the more riveted we become to its content and the more we identify with it.

The Scriptures tell us that Jesus taught about anxiety. Matthew records a lengthy portion on worry in the Sermon on the Mount. He mentions it four times in ten verses between Matthew 6:25 and Matthew 6:34. In that section Jesus admonishes us to stop worrying about our physical needs and, instead, trust God to meet them. He Himself experienced the full range of human emotions from pleasant ones like joy to unpleasant ones like the anguish He felt in the garden of Gethsemane just prior to His arrest and crucifixion (Matt. 26).

Prominent characters in the Old Testament such as Adam and Eve, Elijah, Job, David, and Moses experienced these same unpleasant emotions. Jeremiah is even called the Weeping Prophet because he wept when he pronounced judgment on the people (Jer. 9:1).

Anxiety, worry, and fear often appear in the pages of Scripture, perhaps because they affect us all. I've often struggled with these. My anxiety has felt like how the Old English writers translated the word *worry*, "to strangle." Anxiety can strangle our joy, peace, and the rest of the fruits of the Spirit from us.

Worry and anxiety form two sides of the same coin.[8] They engage our brain's fight-or-flight center in similar ways. Psychologists call this process repetitive negative thinking. We worry with our minds when we expect problems or imagine vague threats that might exist in the future. We get anxious about our emotions when we feel those problems or threats might pounce on us. Worry is more thought-based while anxiety relates more to bodily sensations and emotions.

Because genetics influences personality, some of us feel negative emotions more often and more easily than others.[9] Science tells us that a happiness "set point" is hardwired into our brains from birth. Some people will experience more happiness than others because their genes predispose them toward it. These people show more activity in the part of the brain activated by positive emotions, the left prefrontal cortex (the area located roughly behind your left temple).[10] The right frontal cortex activates more often for those who frequently feel sad.[11] However, as the Holy Spirit transforms us, our set points can change.[12] We can experience greater joy and happiness. The practices can help us change our happiness set points.

## Brain Insight on Emotions

Neuroscience tells us that emotions play a significant role in stress resilience. Your capacity to regulate your emotions in God-honoring ways rises when your resilience rises.[13] The following section highlights key brain insights on emotions and stress resilience.

Compassion fatigue worsens the stress response. Compassion fatigue happens when, as you try to meet other people's needs, the extent or time commitment required becomes exhausting. This results in negative effects from stress that can lead to burnout and more unpleasant emotions. However, researchers have found that we can minimize the negative effects that come when we serve others by focusing on Jesus.[14]

Chronic stress weakens the connections between the part of the brain that controls our emotions (the pre-frontal cortex) and a key part involved in the fear response (the amygdala). When we don't respond to stress in a healthy way, our emotions can override clear thinking.[15] Such stress narrows our physical and psychological field of view, and we don't see options and resources that could help us. Chronic stress biases our thinking toward negativity.[16]

Positive affect (a general term for overall emotions or mood) contributes to overall wellbeing.[17] Sustained positive affect even reduces inflammation, which science has linked to many diseases, including cancer and heart disease. Positive affect lowers the stress hormone cortisol and enhances our immune system so that we can resist sickness better.[18] When we experience more positive emotions than negative ones and describe life as going relatively well, greater well-being results. This reduces the effects of stress.[19] Positive affect even helps people cope better with situations filled with chronic stress events over which they have no control.[20]

Our emotions from a prior situation, whether good or bad, often carry over to the next situation. These carry-over emotions don't connect to the present situation. Psychologists label this *sentiment override*. When this happens, we may become defensive or react in an otherwise neutral or positive situation. Our reaction has little to do with the current situation. However, researchers have found that a strong identity in Christ helps us counter unhealthy sentiment override.[21]

Emotion plays a significant role in decision-making because it subconsciously affects the importance we assign to goals and the weight we give to objective information.[22] It helps us make sense of circumstances and feeds our rational thought so that we can make better decisions. The concept, *core affect*, relates to decision-making and works like an internal thermometer that reflects our general sense of well-being. It watches for threats to our body's balancing system, homeostasis. One scientist wrote,

> The goal of mastering the impact of core affect is best achieved by monitoring it, which will enable you to recognize how being cold or tired or hungry or hurting might be having an impact on you and how the same conditions might also be affecting those you interact with. Once you become aware, you can make a conscious effort to avoid situations . . . in which you make bad decisions or have bad personal interactions that could have been avoided.[23]

One well-known study on nuns illustrates how positive emotions affect our well-being and may help us live longer.

> On September 22, 1930, the mother superior of the North American Sisters of Milwaukee, Wisconsin, sent a letter to young nuns in different parts of the country, requesting that they write three-hundred-word essays about their lives. Years later in a longevity study that examined these letters, researchers found that, "The nuns who'd been the most positive lived about ten years longer than those who'd been the least." The nun study helped fuel a new field called positive psychology.[24]

## Best Practice: Notice, Name, and Distance

As a kid I attended a birthday party where the host gave us a Chinese finger trap as a party favor. It's a cheap tube-like toy large enough to put a finger into each end. It "traps" you if you try to pull your fingers out. The harder you try to remove your fingers, the tighter it gets. The only way to free yourself is to loosen the tension on your fingers by gently pushing *into* the tube. In a similar way, if we try to suppress a hard emotion or use the Whac-a-Mole method, the emotion can tighten around our soul.

Just like we remove our fingers from a Chinese finger trap, this practice parallels how we deal with difficult emotions. We must lean in to our emotions rather than stuffing, ignoring, or denying them. Several mini skills described below reinforce Notice, Name, and Distance.

## NOTICE

Notice means that we don't ignore our unpleasant emotions. Rather, we intentionally notice them and lean in to them. The finger trap visualizes that we must release our attempts to force away our unpleasant emotions. As we notice and lean in to them, they will loosen their grip on us. God's grace empowers us to no longer be at their mercy. We notice our emotions in two ways: "learn your emotional processing style" and use the "body scan."

The emotional processing style refers to the unique way we perceive, express, regulate, and respond to our emotions. Psychologists Kirk Strosahl and Patricia Robinson created this simple equation that describes it.

> Our emotional processing style =
> our feeling tone +
> our response tendency +
> our judgment biases.[25]

Stressful situations give us opportunities to learn our processing style. As we become more consistently aware of our style and change how we respond to stress, we can reconfigure our brains' pathways. We become more resilient rather than letting our brains run on autopilot. These questions can help you discover your style

- *Feeling tone*: What does stress physically feel like in your body? My shoulders tighten. For others a headache or stomach pain may reveal their feeling tone.

- *Response tendency*: What do you do immediately when you feel stressed? Do you avoid people, immediately stuff the emotion, or ignore it? I try to control the people or the situation.

- *Judgment biases:* In a stressful situation, what kind of mental commentary do you add to the facts? What themes seem common? I generate worst-case scenarios in my mind.

So, the first mini skill in Notice is "understand your emotional processing style." The second one, learn how to do a "body scan," relates to a process called interoception.[26]

Interoception means the ability God gave us to feel or sense our inner body states. These states include hunger, thirst, emotions, intuition, "gut" feelings, and even our spiritual and relational yearnings. This awareness acts like a gauge to help us better manage our energy and our internal resources in stressful situations. You may feel butterflies in your stomach, anxiety, a fluttering heart, disgust, or warmth.

Researchers have found that interoception plays a significant role in developing resilience. "Resilience is rooted in our awareness of the sensations that originate in our organs and extremities—and the more alert we are to these inner signals, the more resilient we are . . . in the face of life's hardships."[27]

Interoception provides these "body reports" that combine with other information like memories and sensory inputs from our external world. They all integrate into "a single snapshot of our present condition, a sense of 'how I feel' in the moment, as well as a sense of the actions we must take to maintain a state of internal balance."[28]

Our brains lack the capacity to process consciously all the information that assails us every day. However, the brain subconsciously processes significant information. Interoception plays a role. It can help surface subconscious information we may need to heed. It can alert us to pay attention to subtle signals like a sigh, quickened breathing, a fluttering heart, or an unexpected anxious feeling. Resilience deepens as we hone our awareness to these signals through a "body scan."

Years ago, my doctor scheduled a bone scan for me because he thought my bones showed signs of early osteoporosis, a weakening of the bones. The bone scan involved a radioactive injection followed by a full body x-ray. As I lay on the x-ray table, the scanner slowly moved over my entire body from the top of my head to the bottom of my feet as it imaged my skeleton. Fortunately, the tests were negative, but my experience provides a helpful metaphor for the body scan. Here's how to do a body scan.

First, imagine a scanner slowly moving over your body as it takes images. Begin the scan with your left leg and then move to your right leg. Your torso, arms, and head follow. As you scan, mentally pause at various places to become more aware of body sensations you may feel. These signals provide subconscious information about your stress.

A body scan helps you become more attuned to where you hold your stress in your body (e.g., your head, your shoulders, your stomach). As you become aware, you can learn to relax those areas. I mentioned earlier that my stress shows up in my shoulders. A body scan alerts me to hunched shoulders. I then can take specific actions to release that tension. The body scan makes us more aware of body stress so that we can act to reduce it and apply the practices. As you make this a habit (you can do it on the fly or in your devotional time), it helps grow your resilience.

So, the first part of this practice, Notice, helps surface how stress might be internally affecting you. The next step, Name, helps you put words to stress-related emotions and feelings.

## NAME

Even though it may seem counterintuitive, when we name an unpleasant emotion, our brain down-regulates that emotion's potency. When we put our emotions into words, called "affect labeling," it reduces activation in our brain's fight-or-flight center (the amygdala).[29] "The simple act of giving a name to what we're feeling has a profound effect on the nervous system, immediately dialing down the body's stress response."[30] Yet if we suppress, ignore, deny, or stuff them, the brain becomes more sensitive to these difficult emotions. They rebound even stronger.[31]

When we appropriately acknowledge our emotions, we boost our well-being in several ways. We enhance self-efficacy (the belief that we can do what is before us). Our ability to interpret stressful experiences increases. We bring our emotions out of autopilot, "thus giving an opportunity to re-consolidate the experience into a more easily accessed emotion and thus more easily regulated."[32] However, if naming your emotions causes you to ruminate and feel worse, consult a good counselor for help.

Name your emotions in this way. If you feel angry, call it anger. When you feel sad, call it sadness. If you feel anxious, call it anxiety. It's that simple. However, you can take this to the next level to incorporate two dimensions, prolific and granular.[33] *Prolific* means to describe your sensation with as many terms as possible.[34] *Granular* means to choose precise words that describe your emotional sensations. As you grow in how you describe your emotions, you enhance the benefits from affect labeling. In the next section, Distance, you'll learn a technique that makes this process even more effective.

You may face two challenges when you label your emotions. The first entails a concept called emotional labor, when you fake how you feel, when you give "service with a smile" though you feel the opposite. If you've lived or worked in environments for long time periods that contributed to emotional labor, it may be difficult for you to name your emotions.[35]

Another challenge involves a personality trait or condition called alexithymia, when a person has difficulty describing his or her emotions. If you struggle with either of these, a tool called a circumplex may help.

A circumplex pictures emotions on a two-dimensional scale in diagram form. You can download an example here: www.charlesstone.com/stress.

When you feel unpleasant emotions surface, remind yourself that God gave us emotions to experience a full life and to help us respond to threats. When you notice and name them, you reduce their intensity; you think more clearly and you respond more wisely. The last part of Notice, Name, and Distance completes the best practice for Reveal How You Feel.

### DISTANCE

Distancing means to put mental space between yourself and the emotions you feel. You view them like you'd view a scene through a camera viewfinder. The viewfinder provides a third-person perspective. Acceptance and commitment therapy[36] illustrates distancing with a roller-coaster metaphor.

We can view a roller coaster from three perspectives: a participant, a participant-observer, or an observer. If you take the participant perspective, you might sit in the front seat of the roller coaster just to experience the thrill. It's all about the experience. Or you may sit in the middle of the roller coaster as a participant-observer. You experience the thrills, but you also watch how those in front of you experience the ride. Finally, you could choose the observer perspective. You don't ride the coaster. Rather, you stay on the ground and watch the participants and the roller coaster itself.

Distancing is like being the observer on the ground. This perspective creates space between the thinker and the thought, the feeler and the feeling. You can distance in one of three ways. The first way distinguishes a description from an evaluation. A description merely describes an emotion. An evaluation, however, attributes subjective qualities to an emotion. When you describe an emotion you might say, "I am having feelings of fear." If you evaluate it, you might say, "My fear is intolerable." Negative evaluations intensify unpleasant emotions. Descriptions soften their intensity.

A second way to distance is to speak to yourself in the second person and use your name. Replace "I am depressed," with, "Okay, Charles. I see you are experiencing some depressive feelings." This distinction allows you to gain emotional distance by shifting from first person, "I," to "you" or third person "he" or "she."[37] And speaking your name reduces a negative emotion's intensity.[38]

Using first person causes "our stress-response hardware [to fire] releasing adrenaline and cortisol, flooding us with negative emotions, which only serve to further rev up our negative verbal stream."[39] Choosing a third-person perspective, however, shortens the duration of our negative emotions and can keep our mental chatter from fueling a negative emotion. So, when a stress-induced emotion arises, shift your self-talk to the third person.

Another concept, temporal distancing, relates to this third-person perspective approach. It means to use your mind to travel into the future when stressed. "Studies show that when people are going through a difficult experience, asking them to imagine how they'll feel about it ten years from now, rather than tomorrow, can be another remarkably effective way of putting their experience in perspective. Doing so leads people to understand that their experiences are temporary, which provides them with hope."[40]

A final mini skill, journaling, also helps you distance. Psychologist James Pennebaker found that asking people to write about their upsetting experiences for fifteen to twenty minutes, taking the perspective of a narrator, helped them feel better, visit the doctor less, and have a healthier immune function.[41] Journaling helps you view circumstances more objectively, which reduces the emotional intensity from daily stress.[42]

In this chapter you learned to Notice, Name, and Distance negative emotions, the key skill for Practice 2: Reveal How You Feel. The next chapter unpacks the flip side of negative emotions, positive ones. You'll discover how to maximize pleasant experiences and emotions to create upward spirals of more pleasant emotions in Practice 3: Broaden and Build.

## REVIEW

*Big idea:* Resolve unpleasant emotions before chronic stress develops.

*Bible insight:* Scripture illustrates how several biblical characters handled their emotions. Some did well. Some didn't.

*Brain insight:* When you name an unpleasant emotion (called affect labeling), you down-regulate its intensity.

*Best practice:* Notice, Name, and Distance.

## APPLICATION

1. Think about your experience with interoception. What internal signals did you notice? What can you do to become more aware of these signals?

2. Try the body scan each day. Start today and practice it for two minutes. Each day for five straight days add two additional minutes when you do a body scan. Note your experience.

3. Recall a recent experience when a negative emotion got the best of you. Replay that situation in your mind and practice distancing yourself from that emotion. Next time when a painful emotion surfaces, try to distance yourself from it.

If you haven't yet downloaded your Stress Resilience Plan, you can do it at www.charlesstone.com/stress. Continue to add to your plan.

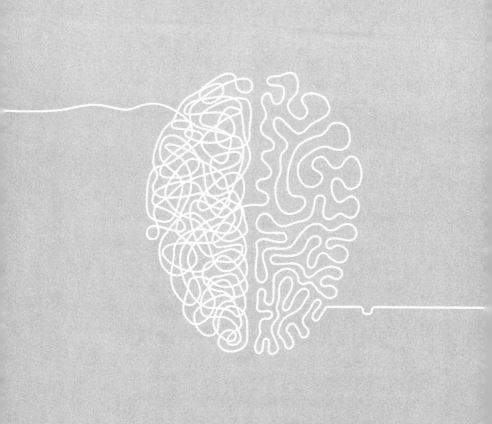

6

# PRACTICE 3:
# Broaden and Build

*Positive emotions fuel resilience.*[1]

**BARBARA FREDRICKSON**
*author and psychologist*

*Burnout is not just about the presence of
negative emotions, but the absence of positive ones.*[2]

**WILLIAM MARTIN MILLER, EDD**

*Big idea:* Increase experiences that satisfy to offset the stress from
experiences that deplete.

*Bible insight:* God gives us pleasant emotions, like joy, to counter
the effects from unpleasant stress-induced emotions.

*Brain insight:* Repeated pleasurable experiences create upward
spirals that foster more pleasurable experiences.

*Best practice:* The Pleasure Piggy Bank.

When I lived in Atlanta several years ago, the green-thumb bug bit
me after I received a seed catalog in the mail. Inside the catalog,

stunning flower photographs mesmerized me. They telegraphed this message, "You, too, can grow flowers like these, but *only* if you buy *our* seeds." After I drooled over the catalog for 37.4 minutes, I got hooked. I ordered $79.83 of Burpee pansy seeds, twenty Styrofoam seed starters with finger-length dirt seed plugs, and a two-foot by eighteen-inch seed warming pad (for special seeds that needed extra TLC).

As I awaited my delivery (this was pre-Amazon next day delivery), I built a large plywood growing table in my basement. I installed a makeshift grow light with a 1,000-watt light bulb my engineer dad gave me. My basement would double as my greenhouse.

For two years I grew flowers from seeds and filled my yard with exquisite purple, yellow, and orange tinted pansies. I convinced myself that I was the envy of the neighborhood . . . until my green-thumb calamity. The third year a plant virus obliterated every single seedling.

That season my green-thumb bug died.

Now I shun flower catalogs and buy pre-planted pansies from Walmart.

My seed-growing experience illustrates Practice 3: Broaden and Build. Broaden and Build is an idea developed by Barbara L. Fredrickson,[3] a college professor and researcher. This concept blends two key ideas. The first states that positive emotions broaden our positive experiences. The second states that those positive emotions build our inner resources to enhance our overall well-being. Positive affect (a general term for mood or emotional state) multiplies positive emotions, broadens thinking, and enhances resilience, like an upward spiral.[4]

The light, water, and fertilizer helped my pansy seeds sprout, grow, and broaden their flower-producing capacity and beauty. Likewise, Broaden and Build states that as we broaden our positive emotional experiences (experiencing more of them), we build inner resources that grow our resilience.

As the process continues, it creates an upward spiral that fosters even more positive experiences that enhance well-being. It also can move in the opposite direction. When we habitually yield to negative thinking and emotions, they drag us into a negativity vortex. Marcus Aurelius, a Roman emperor from AD 161 to 180, captures how sustained negative or positive thoughts affect us with this insight: "The soul becomes dyed with the color of its thoughts."[5]

This chapter covers the flip side of the topic described in the prior chapter. That chapter explained how to minimize the effects from negative affect (emotions). This chapter explains how to amplify positive affect to enhance stress resilience.

Earlier I referred to an amazing study that illustrates how positive emotion, central to Broaden and Build, affects well-being. Author and physicist Dr. Leonard Mlodinow describes that study that expands the illustration here.

On September 22, 1930, the mother superior of the North American Sisters of Milwaukee, Wisconsin, sent a letter to young nuns in different parts of the country, requesting that they write three-hundred-word essays about their lives. Mostly in their early twenties, the nuns were asked to include outstanding and edifying events from their childhood, and influences that led them to the religious life.

The handwritten essays not only contained an accounting of information and feelings; they also reflected, in how they were written, each nun's personality. The essays were eventually filed away, and they sat untouched for decades. Then, sixty years after they were written, they were stumbled upon by a trio of longevity researchers from the University of Kentucky whose work focused on retired nuns.

Amazingly, 180 of the essay writers were among their own research subjects. Sensing an extraordinary opportunity, the scientists analyzed the essays' emotional content, classifying each as positive, negative, or neutral. And then, over the next nine years of their study, they tabulated the correlation between the nuns' personal disposition and their lifespan.

Their conclusion was astonishing: The nuns who'd been the most positive lived about ten years longer than those who'd been the least. The nun study helped fuel a new field called "positive psychology."[6]

This research study illustrates the following biblical insight on how a positive disposition contributes to Broaden and Build.

## Bible Insight on Broaden and Build

The exact phrase, "broaden and build," isn't found in Scripture. However, both the Old and New Testaments reference many dispositions related to joy that help us grow through difficulty.

King David loved God and often faced stressful experiences. Yet the Psalms reflect his confidence that He would sustain him. Every time David obeyed the Lord and trusted Him in that circumstance, He refreshed David's soul with His joy. These verses show how God multiplied David's joy to buffer the negative effects from stress-filled experiences.

- "The Lord is my strength and my shield; my heart trusts in him, and he helps me. My heart leaps for joy" (Ps. 28:7).
- "God is our refuge and strength, an ever-present help in trouble" (Ps. 46:1).
- "When anxiety was great within me, your consolation brought me joy" (Ps. 94:19).
- "The Lord has done it this very day; let us rejoice today and be glad" (Ps. 118:24).
- "The Lord has done great things for us, and we are filled with joy" (Ps. 126:3).

Nehemiah, another biblical character, faced the daunting task to rebuild Jerusalem's walls. As he completed each construction phase, God gave him the inner and outer resources to take the next step. God even exceeded Nehemiah's requests when He prompted King Artaxerxes to provide not only building materials for the project, but a military escort for safe passage to Jerusalem (Neh. 2). Although Nehemiah faced adversaries and obstacles without and critics within, each step led to an upward spiral that built upon a prior successful step. He illustrates "broaden and build" in this famous verse: "The joy of the LORD is your strength" (Neh. 8:10).

The book of Proverbs often tells how pleasant emotions spur us forward, the essence of Broaden and Build.

- "Above all else, guard your heart, for everything you do flows from it" (Prov. 4:23).
- "Those who promote peace have joy" (Prov. 12:20).
- "A happy heart makes the face cheerful" (Prov. 15:13).
- "A cheerful heart is good medicine" (Prov. 17:22).

The apostle Paul embodies Broaden and Build. Although he spent considerable time in prison, he often wrote that the Lord gave him joy in those stressful circumstances. He describes the fruit of the Spirit in Galatians 5:22–33, where he links the idea of positive emotions to constructive attitudes and behaviors. He wrote that Philemon gave him "great joy and encouragement" because he "refreshed the hearts of the Lord's people" (Philem. 1:7).

Perhaps Romans 15:13 best illustrates how Paul echoed Broaden and Build. "May the God of hope fill you with all joy and peace as you trust in him, so that you may overflow with hope by the power of the Holy Spirit" (Rom. 15:13). Paul describes a joy that the Holy Spirit gives in increasing measures when life gets tough.

Paul also reminds us that although we shouldn't create difficulty for ourselves, we shouldn't shy away from it, because difficulty and suffering develop character. He wrote, "We also glory in our sufferings, because we know that suffering produces perseverance; perseverance, character; and character, hope" (Rom. 5:3–4). Neuroscientists have discovered what Paul knew all along. "Exposure to something that causes stress, called stress inoculation, . . . builds resilience. . . . It's a process that toughens us against stress."[7]

## Brain Insight on Broaden and Build

God wired our brains with a fundamental organizing principle: minimize danger/threat and maximize safety/reward.[8] That's why we repeat experiences we enjoy and avoid experiences we don't. Our brains like to feel the positive sensations that a neurotransmitter called dopamine (and other brain chemicals as well) evokes when we experience pleasure, learn something new, or feel motivated.[9]

Sometimes, however, "feel-good" experiences harm us, like using drugs to get a high. However, healthy, "positive affective experiences initiate a cascade of nonconscious processes that may orient [us] to repeat previously enjoyed behaviors."[10] When we "feel good in the present . . . broadening thinking and building resources—positive emotions increase the likelihood that people will feel good in the future."[11] That statement captures the essence of Broaden and Build. Also, when we experience more positive emotions than negative emotions and describe life as going well, our well-being increases. Our joy can increase despite difficulty.

Although more positive emotion is better, Fredrickson cautions that extremely high positive emotion can put people in situations where the negatives outweigh the benefits, like when someone ignores dangerous situations (e.g., trying to take a selfie on a cliff and falling over the edge). Sometimes negative emotions can even motivate us. When we get angry at injustice, it can prompt us to stop it.[12]

Increased positive affect, the cornerstone of Broaden and Build, benefits us in these ways. Positive emotions expand our awareness of options and potential resources that can help us deal with present and future stressful challenges. Positive emotions help us take in more information from our context than we would have absorbed had we been in a neutral or negative emotional state. Negative emotions narrow our thinking. Positive emotions broaden our thinking.

Several positive emotions illustrate Broaden and Build. Joy can create playfulness, which can lead to new ways to problem-solve. Interest can lead us to explore options we might have missed. Contentment can help us savor current experiences and strengthen relationships with those who might help us resolve a current challenge. These recurring emotions create an upward positive spiral as we adapt and build more resources for future challenges.[13]

Positive emotions enhance our thinking, because the increased dopamine levels during positive emotions "enhance consolidation of long-term memory, working memory, creative problem solving, and cognitive flexibility."[14] The inner resources we accrue from positive emotions continue beyond the transient emotion itself. They act as reserves we can draw upon in the future.[15]

Positive emotions increase optimism. "The psychological broadening sparked by one positive emotion can increase an individual's receptiveness to subsequent pleasant or meaningful events, increasing the odds that the individual will find positive meaning in these subsequent events and experience additional positive emotions."[16] Positive emotions help us place stressful events into a larger context, which lessens the impact from a specific negative event.

Overall, positive emotions enhance resilience and general well-being. They help us recover more quickly from negative experiences and build resilience for the next stressful event. This is called the "undoing effect," and it acts as an antidote to the effects unpleasant emotions create.[17]

Fredrickson's research found that positive emotions cut in half the nervous and cardiovascular systems' recovery time from a negative emotion.[18] Positive emotions can "undo" the negative effects from stress-inducing situations. A way to foster positive emotions might be to interject humor at the right moment when you feel stressed.

Upward spirals from positive emotions broaden our thinking, build inner resources, and trigger even more spirals to boost our stress resilience.

## Best Practice: The Pleasure Piggy Bank

When we were kids, we all had piggy banks. Often made of porcelain, the pig-shaped bank included a slot at the top where we could drop in our allowance or money from the tooth fairy. It was a kid's version of a savings account. The more coins we deposited, the more "wealthy" we became. In a similar fashion, God created us with a *joy piggy bank*. The more joy coins (activities and choices that honor God, give Him pleasure, and bless others) that we put into that bank, the richer in resilience we become.[19] Of course, those coins must fall within biblical parameters. They are not all about worldly pleasures. Accumulated joy coins, however, illustrate Broaden and Build.

A study of almost five hundred female twins found when people build pleasurable experiences into their day, what we might call patches of pleasure (the coins), resilience deepens.[20] Doing this triggers our reward system and motivates us.[21] God wired our brains to desire reward and to feel motivated to behave in certain ways. Three components motivate us toward reward experiences: wanting, liking, and learning.

Neuro-ophthalmologist Dr. Mithu Storoni explains it this way:

- Wanting: When you anticipate pleasure, your reward circuit fires and motivates you to reach for it.

- Liking: When a thing or a person or a situation makes you feel pleasure, your reward circuit fires.
- Learning: You learn that performing an action leads to feeling pleasure and you know that to perform this action again will give pleasure.[22]

Identifying those pleasures is the "learning" part. Putting them on the calendar leads to anticipation and "wanting" more of them. Gratefulness for them, as you experience them, would equate to "liking" them. And no matter how stressful your day, a reward experience can confer a bit of resilience on us.

However, these experiences don't happen on their own. It takes effort and intention to plan them into our day and to see them when they come. A therapy for depression called "Engage" helps clients choose activities and action steps to increase rewarding experiences.[23] Even if you don't struggle with depression, this idea applies to our pleasure piggy bank. When you take steps to schedule pleasant emotions into your day, the pleasure coins that result will enhance resilience.

Here's how to apply this best practice. Include at least three pleasurable activities into your daily schedule. If you've lost joy in these activities (a term called anhedonia), write the reasons you feel that way. Alongside those negative reasons, write two counterarguments. Do this daily for about two weeks and you'll develop habits that will increase the pleasure coins in your pleasure piggy bank.

What might qualify as pleasure coins? Any of these activities could: mindfulness practice (noticing, with a holy purpose, God, His creation, and our inner world of thoughts and feelings), music, a walk in a park, acting on a task you have control over, exercise, a hobby, singing, laughter, or spending time with family and friends. Consider even small daily experiences like a cup of warm tea as a pleasure coin. Remember, God designed us to enjoy Him, others, and His creation. Jesus said that He came to give us joy and an abundant life (John 10:10). Pleasure is a gift from Him. Paul wrote, "[God] richly provides us with everything for our enjoyment" (1 Tim. 6:17).

In this chapter, you've learned about Practice 3: Broaden and Build. As we experience more positive emotions (affect), we broaden our thinking, discover new resources, and stimulate more positive experiences. As we increase the deposits into our pleasure piggy banks, we will nurture Broaden and Build upward cycles that will grow our resilience.

In the next chapter, we'll look more deeply into how healthy thinking enhances resilience in Practice 4: Audit Your Thoughts.

## REVIEW

*Big Idea:* Increase experiences that satisfy to offset the stress from experiences that deplete.

*Bible insight:* God gives us pleasant emotions, like joy, to counter the effects from unpleasant stress-induced emotions.

*Brain insight:* Repeated pleasurable experiences create upward spirals that foster more pleasurable experiences.

*Best practice:* The Pleasure Piggy Bank.

## APPLICATION

1. Reflect on a recent experience that fostered pleasant emotions. How did that experience broaden your perspective or thinking at that moment?

2. With the pansy-growing analogy in mind, recall an instance when you nurtured a pleasant emotion that led to "broadening and building" your personal resilience. What did that experience feel like? How did it motivate you to repeat it?

3. List three to five patches of pleasure/joy coins, activities or practices that bring you joy.

4. Which of these "pleasure coins" could you more frequently deposit into your pleasure piggy bank? List three steps you could take this week to increase your pleasure bank account.

5. Reflect on the nun study. What correlation do you see between your emotional experiences and your overall well-being?

Continue adding to your Stress Resilience Plan.

For downloadable tools, visit this web link: www.charlesstone.com/stress.

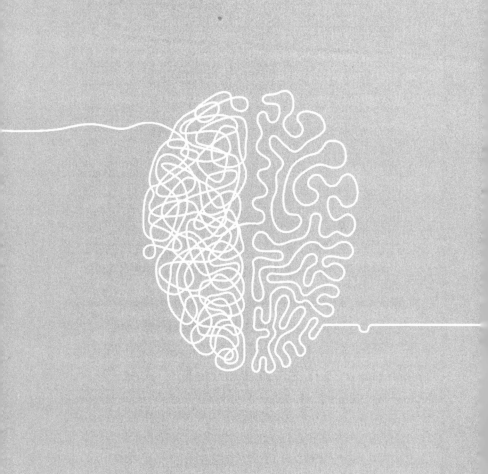

7

## PRACTICE 4:
# Audit Your Thoughts

*I've had a lot of worries in my life,
most of which never happened.*

**MARK TWAIN**

*(1835–1910)*

*Big idea:* Reinforce positive thoughts and redirect negative ones to fortify your resilience.

*Bible insight:* Authentic spiritual transformation requires a transformed mind.

*Brain insight:* If we appraise an experience as stressful, even though it isn't, it probably will become stressful.

*Best practice:* The START cognitive control process.

Fun (or not so fun) facts about your thinking.

- Thoughts race through our brain at about 250 miles per hour.
- We think more than 6,000 thoughts per day, one thought every ten seconds when we're awake.[1]

- 60–70 percent of our thoughts turn negative and relate to inferiority, love and approval, or control-seeking.[2]
- Our brains wander 47 percent of our waking time to thoughts unrelated to our current tasks.[3]
- A wandering mind leads to an unhappy mind.[4]

These facts illustrate that negative thinking comes at us fast and furious. Unless we attend to this tendency and alter our thinking, negative thoughts will inevitably increase stress. In this chapter you'll learn how to replace stress-induced thinking with resilience-building thinking. Practice 4: Audit Your Thoughts can help you form healthy thinking patterns.

## Bible Insight on Our Thinking

Scripture says much about our thinking. The NIV translation uses the word *mind(s)* or *think* more than 280 times. King David asked the Lord to examine not only his heart but his mind as well (Ps. 139:23–24). Matthew reminds us to love Jesus with our minds (Matt. 22:37). A key theological word for repentance, *metanoia*, means to *change our minds*. The apostle Paul used *mind* almost fifty times. The following verses (with italics added) highlight his key ideas about the mind.

"Set your *minds* on things above, not on earthly things" (Col. 3:2).

"We have the *mind* of Christ" (1 Cor. 2:16).

"Finally, brothers and sisters, whatever is true, whatever is noble, whatever is right, whatever is pure, whatever is lovely, whatever is admirable—if anything is excellent or praiseworthy—*think* about such things" (Phil. 4:8).

In the Old Testament, Joshua admonishes us to engage our minds when we read Scripture. "Keep this Book of the Law always on your lips; meditate on it day and night, so that you may be careful to do everything written in it" (Josh. 1:8). When we repeat the same thoughts (e.g., when we read, contemplate, or study Scripture), we evoke neuroplasticity. In an earlier chapter I defined neuroplasticity as "the ability of the nervous system to respond to intrinsic or extrinsic stimuli by reorganizing its structure, function and connections."[5] Even though the writers of the Bible didn't understand this concept, we can apply it in our lives today.

Neuroplasticity strengthens our brain circuits around our thoughts, whether they are good or bad ones. Fortunately, this God-given ability empowers us to reconfigure wrong thinking much like a river diverts its flow. First, parallel to the river, a tiny trickle may appear. Then a small stream develops. As it continues to flow, it deepens its channel and widens its borders. A large creek then forms. As this process continues, it eventually becomes a river. If water keeps feeding into it, it will develop into a mighty river. The former channel still exists, but it lacks its former power. The new channel now holds the power because the water flows through it.

Neuroplasticity acts similarly. As you repeatedly engage Scripture, new healthy thinking circuits form in your mind. This remapping doesn't happen all at once, but as new circuits slowly form, the old ones gradually become less prominent. When we alter our thinking patterns, we divert our thought life from unhealthy and sometimes sinful thoughts to wholesome, beneficial, and redemptive ones. As the Holy Spirit creates these new rivers of truth, we experience more joy and stress resilience grows. He re-zones our brains to give greater cognitive real estate to life-giving thoughts rather than to draining ones.

The apostle Paul describes this process as a transformed mind. "Do not conform to the pattern of this world, but be transformed by the renewing of your mind" (Rom. 12:2). As you apply the skills in this chapter, the Holy Spirit will transform your mind.

## Brain Insight on Our Thinking

Our thinking process receives information from multiple sources. "Your senses give your brain input regarding the environment; your memory provides information about the past; your knowledge base and beliefs ground you with regard to how the world works."[6]

Chronic stress erodes that thinking process in several ways. It worsens the negativity bias, our brains' bias to default to negative thinking. Our brains constantly scan for bad news. When they find it, they focus on it and lose sight of the big picture. This bias also causes us to overreact to bad news and more easily insert negative thoughts into memory.[7] Chronic stress also enhances neuronal growth in our brains' fight-or-flight centers. This exacerbates the harmful effects from stress-evoking thinking.[8]

Stress weakens memory because it shrinks the neurons in our primary memory control center, the hippocampus. It can even destroy neurons if stress becomes chronic.[9] Stress further affects memory by inhibiting our ability to put memories into long-term memory.[10] We can't learn unless new information solidifies in long-term memory so that we can later recall and use what we learned.

Stress impairs how well our high-level thinking center, the pre-frontal cortex (PFC), functions. Our PFC helps us set goals and follow through on them, pay attention, regulate emotions, tolerate stress, and optimize short-term memory.[11] When someone under stress says, "I just can't think," that response shows how stress affects our thinking. Even perceived stress (when we make up stressful scenarios that don't reflect reality) can do the same thing. It slows our brains' processing speed and memory retrieval. It dilutes the accuracy of information we receive and inhibits focus. Thinking itself can even become a chore during stress.[12] Chronic stress even correlates to worsening cognitive effects from Alzheimer's disease.[13]

Stress interferes with attention. Attention affects learning, memory, emotion, perception, decision-making, social interaction, fulfillment, and our sense of accomplishment. It includes both the ability to focus on something and the ability to ignore distractions. It filters out distractions so that we avoid mental overload. However, when attention becomes compromised, we lose many of its helpful functions. Dr. Amishi Jha, professor of psychology and director of contemplative neuroscience at the University of Miami, has extensively studied how attention affects us. She categorizes attention in four ways:

- If you're feeling that you're in a cognitive fog: depleted attention.
- If you're feeling anxious, worried, or overwhelmed by your emotions: hijacked attention.
- If you can't seem to focus so you can take action or dive into urgent work: fragmented attention.
- If you feel out of step and detached from others: disconnected attention.[14]

She notes that stress affects our attention because it creates tunnel vision that narrows perception to the stress/threat that lies in front of us. It biases our attention so that we focus on that threat.[15] And chronic stress diminishes our ability to draw the insight from our world that we need to make wise decisions.[16] It narrows choices and makes us more likely to make risky, unhealthy, or irrational ones.

So, stress can impair our thought lives. The best practice below, START, overlaps the first two steps in the STOPP process you learned in chapter 4 on Practice 1: Cease and Breathe. However, this practice helps you build stress reliance through changed thinking.

## Best Practice: START Cognitive Control Process

Our brain's working memory limits how much information we can process at once and limits how much moves to long-term memory, called memory consolidation. A brain hack called *chunking* helps increase that capacity. When we pack more information into easily recalled words or phrases, we *chunk*. In grammar school you did this when you learned the names of the Great Lakes with the word HOMES. Each letter cued you to a lake's name, H for Lake Huron, O for Ontario, M for Michigan, E for Erie, and S for Superior. Just as HOMES helped you recall the names of the Great Lakes, the word START can do the same for each step of the practice. You already saw that I used chunking in STOPP, the best practice for Practice 2: Reveal How You Feel. You'll see chunking in later chapters as well. Here's what the letters in START represent.

S: **S**top

T: **T**ake a breath

A: **A**udit your thoughts

R: **R**eappraise reality

T: **T**ransition your attention

### S: STOP

In chapter 4, I explained the S for "Stop" and prefaced it with a section on the ancient practice statio. As a refresher, statio is the discipline of taking brief stops during the day before starting a new task. It allows us to break our hurry, focus on the Lord, respond to stress, get closure from the prior task, and prepare our hearts and minds for what comes next.

This same skill applies for the first step in START. Refresh your memory by rereading that section in chapter 4.

### T: TAKE A BREATH

I also covered this step in chapter 4 when I described the breath prayer. Deep breathing engages the vagus nerve, the brain's emotional brake, which calms the stress response. So, the first T in START means to take a few deep breaths when you feel stress to engage your brain's calming system. I suggest rereading that section as well.

## A: AUDIT YOUR THOUGHTS

Next, through a concept called metacognition, you audit your thoughts. The word for this practice, metacognition,[17] means to think about your thinking.[18] It's the ability to step back and take a third-person perspective on your thoughts and "observe" your thinking. In educational circles it also applies to how a person solves problems or learns new information. This mental monitoring "is not difficult, but, like improving your posture, it requires continual effort."[19] You might call this "check your chatter" or "pay attention to what you are paying attention to." It's as simple as asking yourself, "What am I thinking about right now?"

This practice can be challenging because often we don't want to face or be left alone with our thoughts. In a Harvard University study, college-aged research participants sat in a room and entertained themselves only with their thoughts.[20] They could think about anything they wanted to. However, they couldn't bring anything into the lab room that provided entertainment . . . no phone, no books, and no writing materials. In the experiment the researchers placed an electrode on the subjects' ankles. They attached the electrode to a battery and a switch that allowed the students to self-administer a mild electrical shock. Several did (67 percent of men and 25 percent of women). Rather than simply "being with" their thoughts, they shocked themselves. The researchers concluded that many people would rather avoid only being with their thoughts, even if they replaced their thinking with something potentially harmful.

This practice is also challenging because we constantly daydream and internally chatter to ourselves. It's called the default mode.[21] We stay in this mode a third to a half of our waking time.[22] Our inner conversation gets so verbose that one study found this verbal stream equaled speaking four thousand words per minute out loud.[23] To put this into perspective, the length of an average State of the Union Address is about six thousand words.

One key study on the wandering mind found that what we think about in the moment better predicts our happiness than what we do in the moment.[24] And continual chatter prolongs our stress response[25] and can even cause harmful inflammation. This chatter "trigger[s] the expression of inflammation genes, which are meant to protect us in the short term but cause harm in the long term."[26]

PhD professor Ethan Kross describes how unabated negative chatter affects thinking.

> Our labor-intense executive functions need every neuron they can get, but a negative inner voice hogs our neural capacity. Verbal rumination concentrates our attention narrowly on the source of our emotional distress, thus stealing neurons that could better serve us. In effect, we jam our executive functions up by attending to a "dual task"—the task of doing whatever it is we want to do and the task of listening to our pained inner voice. Neurologically, that's how chatter divides and blurs our attention.[27]

It sabotages our ability to focus on a task.

The goal in Audit Your Thoughts is not to stop all inner chatter. We can't. God designed our brains this way. Rather, we should strive to more often notice our thoughts, assess their helpfulness, and change them if they're not helpful or God-honoring. The next two steps help us do that.

When you audit your thoughts, you use metacognition to pay attention to what you are paying attention to. Again, it's as simple as asking yourself, "Right now, what am I thinking about?" These thoughts might be retrospective, a rehash over something painful in the past. They might show up as a prospective thought, worry about something in the future. When you run mental simulations about a past experience or a future fear, you clog up your brain's operating capacity. This step in the START skill can help unclog your brain's cognitive machinery.

So, Audit Your Thoughts is the third step in the best practice, START.

However, don't overdo this introspective look. Unhealthy introspection can backfire. It can undermine performance, strain relationships, hamper decision-making, degrade mental health, and hinder moral thinking.[28]

## R: REAPPRAISE THINKING

When we feel stress, our thoughts and emotions get skewed and often they don't reflect reality. Even perceiving something as stressful can engage the brain's stress response.[29] Pastors are especially vulnerable to this. One study found that perceived church demands contributed more to pastoral burnout than did actual demands.[30] One author called this unfounded fear *paper tiger paranoia*,[31] overestimating threats and underestimating our ability to handle them.

A positive reappraisal style helps us fight rumination. Rumination involves the old material of life when we obsessively replay past events in our minds.[32] Its cousin, worry, involves new material, what might happen. Worry and rumination engage the front part of our brain (PFC), yet as we habitually reappraise, we can consistently turn down our brains' fear center, the amygdala.[33] One research team noted that all the resilience factors that protect us against stress converge through reappraisal.[34]

Three data sources combine in reappraisal: the stimulus that created the stress (e.g., a conflict), our memories that recall similar situations, and the actual reappraisal of that situation. We reappraise in three ways.

*1. Objectively evaluate the situation.*

When you feel stress, first ask yourself questions like these. "How big is the threat?" "How likely is it to happen?" "How bad would it be if it happened?"[35] These questions can help you align your thinking with reality.

*2. Keep perspective.*

One meta-analysis examined emotion-regulation strategies and found that perspective-taking proved very effective in emotional control.[36] A mountain visualizes how we can keep perspective. Our thoughts and emotions are much like weather that constantly surrounds a mountain. It includes bad weather like heavy rain and lightning, as well as pleasant weather like cool breezes and sunshine. To quote Martin Laird, "The mountain does not become the weather. It simply observes it."[37]

King David penned these words about Mount Zion, "Those who trust in the LORD are like Mount Zion, which cannot be shaken but endures forever" (Ps. 125:1). As Laird writes, "Mt Zion symbolizes God's power, blessing, and protection." When in stressful situations "we trust in the Lord and redirect our thinking and our attention," we take on attributes of a mountain. Just as a mountain does not become the weather surrounding it, we don't become our stressful thoughts and emotions, our internal weather. Rather, we observe them and then we reappraise them. "In Christ we are like that mountain with all kinds of . . . internal weather." We may prefer certain kinds of internal weather (i.e., pleasant emotions), but we are not the weather.[38] Yet because we are hidden in Christ in God, He is our rock, our fortress, and our foundation. We rely on Him when we experience difficult thoughts and emotions, unpleasant internal weather. And as bad weather around a mountain will eventually pass, so, too, will our unpleasant internal weather pass.

So, step two in Audit Your Thoughts is to keep perspective.

*3. Reframe the stress-inducing experience as a challenge rather than a threat.*

A belief that we have control in stressful situations buffers us against stress.[39] Even a mere perception of control (when there is none) can be helpful.[40]

Psychologists say that we ask ourselves two questions when we face stress.

What is required of me in these circumstances, and do I have the personal resources to cope with what's required? If we scan the situation and conclude that we don't have the wherewithal needed to handle things, that leads us to appraise the stress as a threat. If, on the other hand, we appraise the situation and determine that we have what it takes to respond adequately, then we think of it as a challenge. Which way we choose to talk about the predicament to ourselves makes all the difference for our inner voice.[41]

Scripture reminds us that the Lord will give us everything we need to face any circumstance. "His divine power has given us everything we need for a godly life through our knowledge of him who called us by his own glory and goodness" (2 Peter 1:3). "I can do all this [being content in every circumstance] through him who gives me strength" (Phil. 4:13). So, step three in Audit Your Thoughts means to view the stress-evoking experience as a challenge rather than a threat. We believe this because God's Word says He will provide everything we need to deal with any challenge.

## T: TRANSITION ATTENTION

The last step in START is to transition or turn your attention from the stress-causing experience to something less stressful. It doesn't mean that you ignore the issue. Rather, it means that you choose to redirect your attention elsewhere or place it on something more hopeful in the situation. Where we place our attention matters. Sonya Parker writes, "Whatever you focus your attention on will become important to you even if it's unimportant."[42]

The brain's attentional system parallels the body's physical "core" muscles. Our core muscles influence the entire body. A strong core means a strong body. Likewise, our attentional system acts like our core "cognitive muscle" that builds resilience against stress. As we strengthen our attentional systems, we build our cognitive core. The more aware of where we place our attention and the more flexible we become to transition it elsewhere, the stronger our stress resilience.

When attention gets compromised and misdirected, it can lead to increased conflict with others, misperceptions, and increased performance errors. It creates more stress. Yet the more aware you become about where you've placed your attention, the more your life performance can improve.[43]

You can strengthen your ability to transition attention in two ways.

First, practice mindfulness. We often get stuck in negative thinking, which increases cognitive clutter and makes threats seem like flashing neon signs. Yet we can train our attention to focus on qualities like truthfulness, purity, loveliness, and excellence that the apostle Paul wrote about in Philippians 4:8. Biblical mindfulness can train our attention.[44] It can help us become more present in the moment so that we can better pay attention to where we've placed our attention and shift it if needed. If you'd like to learn about biblical mindfulness, consider my book *Holy Noticing: The Bible, Your Brain, and the Mindful Space Between Moments* to learn a biblical approach to mindfulness.

Second, rest your attention. It's a science-based practice called attention restoration theory.[45] This concept says that we can divide attention into two types, involuntary and voluntary or directed attention. Involuntary attention happens naturally when something surprising or novel captures our attention. But since attention is a finite resource, repeated use tires it and creates mental fatigue. Directed attention means that we choose to redirect attention to something else to rest and restore it. In other words, when we take a break from focusing on a stressful situation, we boost our inner resources to help us deal with the issue better.

Restorative environments can provide cognitive quietness to restore our attention. A restorative environment includes four traits. The first is physical and/or mental distance from the stress-inducing situation. Trait two involves sufficient time away from it. The third entails fascination with the new environment or activity that sufficiently intrigues us so that we don't need to use our cognitive capacity to reject distractions. Trait four is a setting where we can do what we want to do.

Settings with all four characteristics might include retreats, places of worship, nature, and vacation destinations that can help restore our attentional abilities. However, they need not require significant time or distance away. The key is regularity. Include restorative habits into your daily, weekly, and annual routines. Daily might involve micro-breaks as simple as looking out a window. They could include a walk in nature, a cup of coffee in a café, or even looking at nature pictures on your computer screen. Weekly might include a Sabbath day of rest or an out-of-town drive to a natural setting. Annual attention rests would include retreats and vacations.[46] When attention works well, we can "focus when we need to, notice when we need to, and plan and manage our behavior when we need to."[47]

In this chapter on Practice 4: Audit Your Thoughts, you learned what the Bible and brain science says about our thinking. You've also learned a key best practice, the START cognitive control process, along with several application tips. The next chapter highlights how we can develop stress resilience when we deepen our relationship with the Lord.

## REVIEW

*Big idea:* Reinforce positive thoughts and redirect negative ones to fortify your resilience.

*Bible insight:* Authentic spiritual transformation requires a transformed mind.

*Brain insight:* If we appraise an experience as stressful, even though it isn't, it probably will become stressful.

*Best practice:* The START cognitive control process.

## APPLICATION

1. When you feel stressed this week, practice metacognition. Think about what you are thinking about and assess if you need to redirect your thinking.

2. This week when you notice an unhelpful stress-induced thought, apply the START model to that thought.

3. Record activities, objects, or sensory noise that distract you. What specific steps could you take to create a more distraction-free environment?

Continue to add to your Stress Resilience Plan.

For downloadable tools, visit this web link: www.charlesstone.com/stress.

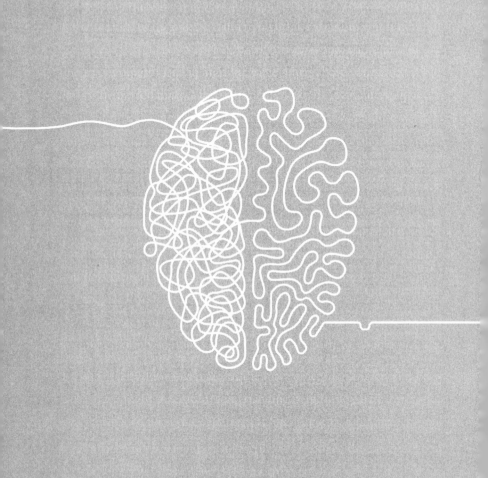

# PRACTICE 5:
# Soak Your Soul

*When we care for our souls,
we are more able to cope with the stresses of life
because we are anchored in God's peace.*

**JOHN ORTBERG**
*author*

*Big idea:* Nurture your soul to combat the stress that stems from spiritual dryness.

*Bible insight:* Spiritual formation lies at the core of stress resilience.

*Brain insight:* Research shows that spiritual disciplines can dampen the stress response.

*Best practice:* The four concepts reflected in CASI.

What images come to mind when you read the words *barrenness, desolation,* and *dryness?*

A withered plant?

A parched desert bed?

A field of brown cornstalks?

A dry well in the hot African bush?

An emaciated dog wandering the freeway?

How your spiritual life sometimes feels?

Every Christian has occasionally experienced spiritual dryness. Research tells us that it contributes to stress[1] and even makes us more prone to perceive situations as stressful.[2]

King David often wrote about his struggle with spiritual dryness. Elijah faced it after his encounter with false prophets (1 Kings 19). Moses' father-in-law told him that unless he reorganized his work responsibilities to lighten his load, he'd burn out (Ex. 18). He heeded the advice. Job's suffering, described in the book of Job, contributed to his.

John of the Cross (1542–91), a Spanish priest, wrote a poem titled "Dark Night of the Soul." The poem describes spiritual dryness as dark periods when God seems remote. Ignatius of Loyola (1491–1556), a Spanish priest, described these dark periods as *desolation*. When we don't sense God's active presence, stress can result.[3]

In more modern times, Oswald Chambers, who authored the devotional *My Utmost for His Highest*, described times when he felt spiritually dry and even depressed. Chambers referred to a four-year-long experience when he "had no conscious communion with Him [God]. The Bible was the dullest, most uninteresting book in existence."[4] Charles Spurgeon and Jonathan Edwards both struggled with spiritual dryness.[5]

This chapter offers practical steps to combat spiritual dryness. These insights can enhance your stress resilience as you soak your soul with biblical truth and with a warm relationship with Jesus.

Intimacy with God reduces stress and minimizes the potential burnout from spiritual dryness.[6] Time with God is one of the best ways to develop stress resilience.[7] One researcher said, "There is an emerging connection between Christian spiritual practices and coping with stress, worry, and burnout."[8]

In prior chapters I included a specific section on Scripture about that chapter's practice. In this chapter, I've sprinkled Scripture throughout the best practices section rather than in a dedicated section. However, it's helpful to begin with this brief biblical perspective on spiritual dryness and how the Lord quenches our spiritual thirst.

- "As the deer pants for streams of water, so my soul pants for you, my God. My soul thirsts for God, for the living God. When can I go and meet with God?" (Ps. 42:1–2).
- "You, God, are my God, earnestly I seek you; I thirst for you, my whole being longs for you, in a dry and parched land where there is no water" (Ps. 63:1).
- "Blessed are those who hunger and thirst for righteousness, for they will be filled" (Matt. 5:6).
- "On the last and greatest day of the festival, Jesus stood and said in a loud voice, 'Let anyone who is thirsty come to me and drink. Whoever believes in me, as Scripture has said, rivers of living water will flow from within them'" (John 7:37–38).

## Brain Insight on Soul Care

Recent research has found that certain spiritual practices can enhance stress resilience. A healthy spiritual life is the number-one predictor of how well we cope with future stress.[9] This chapter won't cover every spiritual practice because this book is not primarily a discipleship book. However, it includes practices that research ties to enhanced stress resilience and overall well-being.

Reflection, biblical meditation, and Christian mindfulness practices can improve physical health. Heart rate variability (HRV), the variation in the time interval between consecutive heartbeats (not the heart rate itself), measures overall health. Meditation-type practices (for believers that means reflecting on God and His Word) improve HRV.[10] Meditation also enhances resilience and decreases perceived stress[11] while promoting stress self-regulation.[12] It even decreases inflammation, which is linked to many serious diseases.[13]

Pastoral leaders struggle with stress, as we all do. One study of pastors found that a weak spiritual life predicted disengagement from others, a component of burnout.[14] Another pastors' study found that reflective, mindful spiritual practices did the opposite. They decreased the stress response and improved the participants' overall quality of life.[15] Studies among pastors show that spiritual disciplines enhance emotional and spiritual health, improve ability to cope with stress, and help pastors avoid burnout.[16] Another study showed that spiritual resources lowered stress and enhanced quality of life more than any other factor.[17] These same findings would apply to any believer, not just to pastors.

Reflective, mindful spiritual practices can enhance moral reasoning and decision making. When we shift our perspective from the subjective and emotional to the objective and thoughtful, we become more mindful of the needs of others.[18] Such a shift helps us apply the scriptural admonition to put others first, "in humility value others above yourselves" (Phil. 2:3). When we do this, we live out a biblical worldview. Conversely, weak theological beliefs make us more susceptible to stress, because we lack a strong spiritual foundation that provides wisdom for moral decision making. One study of ministry leaders found that those who lacked a solid, integrated set of beliefs struggled to find the inner foundation for ministry, which resulted in stress.[19]

When we neglect our spiritual life, we miss a key resource that builds stress resilience. The section below uses the acronym CASI to explain four key spiritual concepts and practices that help us apply this chapter's practice, Soak Your Soul.

A caution is in order, though. We should not practice these spiritual disciplines simply to improve our resilience. Rather, we should practice them primarily to help us conform to Christ's image. Dallas Willard wrote, "They [spiritual disciplines] train us for leading the life that God intended for us: one that has the power and character to fulfill our calling. They are methods by which we obey the command to 'put off' the old person and to 'put on' the new person who is in the likeness of Christ (Col. 3:9–10; Eph. 4:22–24)."[20]

## Best Practice: CASI

The acronym CASI embodies four spiritual practices that help us soak our souls with the Word and person of Christ.

- Collaboration: Problem-solve with God.
- Awe: Deepen daily worship.
- Sabbath: Practice weekly Sabbath.
- Identity: Cultivate Christ-based identity.

### COLLABORATION: PROBLEM-SOLVE WITH GOD

Every day, problems and choices require our decisions. Some decisions lack significance (the color of the socks you pick). Others carry great consequences ("Will I click on a link that may send me to a porn site?"). The choices we make influence the stresses we face. A Spirit-based problem-solving approach improves decision making and enhances stress resilience. Dr. Kenneth I. Pargament, professor emeritus of psychology at Bowling Green State University, proposed an idea that describes three ways we spiritually cope with stressful circumstances. He calls this concept religious coping theory.[21]

The first way we make decisions he calls the *collaborative coping style*. In this style, the person works in unison with God, who helps them find solutions to problems, rather than viewing God as distant and uninvolved. Believers collaborate with God, rather than resisting or ignoring Him. They view stressful situations through a spiritual lens as they seek God's direction through His Word. God guides and the person takes responsibility to problem-solve in God-honoring ways. This person draws upon spiritual resources. As a result, this style shows the person experiences a secure connection to God and others. Pargament calls this *positive religious coping.*

Pargament calls the second style *self-directing coping.* These people count on themselves to find the solution. They go it alone and don't include God in the decision-making process. They rely on their own strengths and abilities. He calls the third style the *deferring coping style.* The person who uses this style waits for God to show them the solution.[22] They do little, stall, and hope God intervenes. Of course, sometimes we must wait on God for direction. However, the last two styles reflect those with a less secure relationship with God. Pargament categorizes these two styles as *negative religious coping.*

His research notes that the first style, *collaborative coping,* helps us best deal with stress. The *deferring style* increases anxiety. The *self-directing style* may help in situations where a person has actual control, but it isn't effective in situations that lie outside their control.[23] People who choose this style rely on their personal resources, whereas the collaborative style looks to God for wisdom and direction while not neglecting their own skills, knowledge, and experience. When in a stressful situation, they can tolerate ambiguity to find the best way forward as they partner with God. The *collaborative style* is "associated with resilience, perceived control, and enhanced self-esteem and confidence to manage difficulties."[24]

So how do you know your dominant coping style? Pargament created a psychometrically sound (valid) inventory called the brief RCOPE inventory (religious coping) composed of the fourteen statements below.[25] The first seven show a positive coping style (collaboration between you and God). The last seven show a negative coping style (relying on yourself or passively waiting for God to intervene). Based on these fourteen statements, evaluate how you respond to stressful circumstances. If your responses align more with the last seven, reflect on the first seven and try to apply those responses the next time you face stress.

Collaborative problem-solving style (positive coping):

1. Looked for a stronger connection with God.
2. Sought God's love and care.
3. Sought help from God in letting go of my anger.
4. Tried to put my plans into action together with God.
5. Tried to see how God might be trying to strengthen me in this situation.
6. Asked forgiveness for my sins.
7. Focused on my faith to stop worrying about my problems.

Self-directing or Deferring Style (negative coping):

1. Wondered whether God had abandoned me.
2. Felt punished by God for my lack of devotion.
3. Wondered what I did for God to punish me.
4. Questioned God's love for me.
5. Wondered whether my church had abandoned me.
6. Decided the devil made this happen.
7. Questioned the power of God.

## AWE: DEEPEN DAILY WORSHIP

Worship, private and corporate, can reduce stress. We worship when we mentally make ourselves less and make God greater in our minds and hearts. We worship when we show Him deep respect, reflect on His holiness, and recognize His transcendence. True worship evokes "awe" of God.

Scientists have found that "awe" that results from experiences like worship provides a hedge against stress.[26] Awe causes an immediate decline in stress by calming our brains' stress response.[27] Awe also reduces pro-inflammatory cytokines, chemical substances in our blood that indicate inflammation.[28] Inflammation that doesn't "turn off" when it should contributes to serious disease such as diabetes, liver disease, cancer, and Alzheimer's.[29]

Neuroscientist Ethan Kross defines *awe* this way: "Awe is the wonder we feel when we encounter something powerful that we can't easily explain. We are often flooded by it in the natural world when we see an incredible sunset, [a] mile-high mountain peak, . . . [a] beautiful view. Awe is considered a self-transcendent emotion in that it allows people to think and feel beyond their own needs and wants. This is reflected in what happens in the brain during awe-inspiring experiences."[30]

The awe we experience in worship, whether in a worship service, while we marvel at God's creation of a sunset, or in a devotional time, reduces our self-interest. It reminds us of our connection with God and other believers. Worship and the awe that results broaden our perspectives on life and lessen our self-focused concerns, which reduces stress.[31]

When you truly worship, you not only bring joy to God's heart and yours, but you lower your stress as well.

## SABBATH: PRACTICE WEEKLY SABBATH

A regular Sabbath rhythm and practice provides another powerful spiritual practice that enhances stress resilience. In the creation account in Genesis, God set aside, blessed, and called the seventh day, the Sabbath, holy (Gen. 2:3). God's covenant with His people included a day of rest (Ex. 31:16). This day reminded the Hebrews to keep a right relationship with God, others, and His creation. The word *Sabbath* literally means to rest, cease, or stop work.[32] The Sabbath day would stand in stark contrast to the brutal work pace the Egyptians forced the Hebrews to keep.

The New Testament expanded Sabbath practice through the life and teaching of Jesus and transitioned the Saturday Sabbath to Sunday with Christ's resurrection. He modeled for us a rhythm of work and rest. He became our Sabbath rest (Heb. 4). Rather, Christ's work on the cross became the way to God. He satisfied the demands of the law once and for all. "Christ approached Sabbath in freedom, noting that the Sabbath is created for people, not as a system of oppression and rules ([see] Mark 2:27–28)."[33]

In Jesus' work with the disciples, ministry needs outstripped the disciples' capacity to meet them. As their exhaustion mounted, Jesus knew they needed self-care. So He told them to rest. "Then, because so many people were coming and going that they did not even have a chance to eat, he said to them, 'Come with me by yourselves to a quiet place and get some rest'" (Mark 6:31).

The same holds true for us today. A tired body and especially a tired soul magnify the harmful effects from stress. Many studies note that spiritual dryness contributes to emotional exhaustion, one of the three components that lead to burnout.[34]

Research also has found that those who practice Sabbath experience a lower burnout rate than those who don't. Sabbath-keepers have higher spiritual well-being, flourishing positive mental health, and a better quality of life.[35]

However, "Sabbath is much more than just the absence of work, but it is the presence of God; an outlook that nourishes the soul because of the time spent with God and the time spent listening to God."[36] The benefits accrue not simply from taking a day off to rest. Rather, they accrue when you add to that day's experience healthy relational interactions, quietness with God, joyful and fun experiences, and emotional refreshment.[37]

Sabbath helps you soak your soul with Him and lessen the effects of stress. One author notes, "Sabbath requires surrender. If we only stop when we are finished with all our work, we will never stop because our work is never completely done. . . . If we refuse rest until we are finished, we will never rest until we die. Sabbath dissolves the artificial urgency of our days because it liberates us from the need to be finished."[38] Sabbath practice can become a powerful took in your stress resilience toolbox.

## IDENTITY: CULTIVATE CHRIST-BASED IDENTITY

Managing stress hinges on understanding and embodying our identity in Christ, a life rooted in biblical faith and values. Psychiatrist Dr. Murray Bowen pioneered a concept called family systems theory that relates to our identity.[39] His concept described the emotional processes that shape social groups and families and why some people manage stress better.

His theory included eight interrelated concepts. He called the core concept differentiation of self (DoS). DoS is the balance between two drives or needs. The first, togetherness, creates a connection with others. The second, individuality, is the desire to be your own person and make your own choices.[40] People with greater DoS understand their emotions better, and as a result stressful relationships don't overwhelm them. They can manage relational tension that creates stress because they have rooted their identity in their core beliefs and values.

Christian researchers have expanded on this idea with a concept called *differentiation of self in Christ* (DifC). DifC focuses on "basing [our] identity in Christ, as adopted into the family of God via Christ's saving work on the cross. DifC provides the solid basis from which to base [our] identity as a child of God, adopted into Christ's family. As a result, [our] identity is based on Christian values and characteristics."[41]

This Christ-based identity provides a foundation to deal with anxiety and stress. It contrasts with an identity based in performance, people-pleasing, and acceptance from others. It means that we find satisfaction in our identity in an unchanging relationship with Jesus and that we let our values direct our choices.

We see this pictured when John baptized Jesus and God said, "You are my Son, whom I love; with you I am well pleased" (Mark 1:11). Jesus was to base His ministry on His core identity as God's Son. "This experience and participation in the Kingdom of God bases satisfaction and well-being on Christ and not on humanity's works."[42]

When we reflect on our biblical values and live them out, the stress hormone decreases.[43] Author and researcher Kelly McGonigal writes that "writing about personal values makes people feel more powerful, in control, proud, and strong. It also makes them feel more loving, connected, and empathetic toward others. It increases pain tolerance, enhances self-control, and reduces unhelpful rumination after a stressful experience."[44]

With this concept in mind, reflect on what Scripture says about your identity in Him. Romans 8:1–11 includes ten spiritual affirmations about your identity in Christ. Download the Christ-Based Identity Guide here: www.charlesstone.com/stress and read the affirmations every day for five straight days to help ingrain more deeply in your heart who you are in Christ.

In this chapter you learned how to apply Practice 5: Soak Your Soul with the steps in the CASI (Collaboration, Awe, Sabbath, Identity) acronym. In the next chapter I'll unpack Practice 6: Cultivate Certainty. This concept explains how the brain needs certainty about the future to lower the stress response and how we can create more certainty.

## REVIEW

*Big idea:* Nurture your soul to combat the stress that stems from spiritual dryness.

*Bible insight:* Spiritual formation lies at the core of stress resilience.

*Brain insight:* Research shows that spiritual disciplines can dampen the stress response.

*Best practice:* The four concepts reflected in CASI.

## APPLICATION

1. Consider a time when you experienced spiritual dryness. How did that affect your stress? Compare this experience with a time when you felt spiritually full. How did that affect your stress?

2. Which of the components of CASI (Collaboration, Awe, Sabbath, Identity) do you practice regularly? Which practice do you apply the least? What can you do to practice that component more often?

3. What is your coping style? How might a shift toward a more collaborative approach benefit you?

4. Think of a time you experienced deep worship. What was it like? How could you increase such times to experience awe more often?

5. Review the download on your identity in Christ. Which concept should you recall and repeat more often?

Continue to add to your Stress Resilience Plan.

For downloadable tools, visit this web link: www.charlesstone.com/stress.

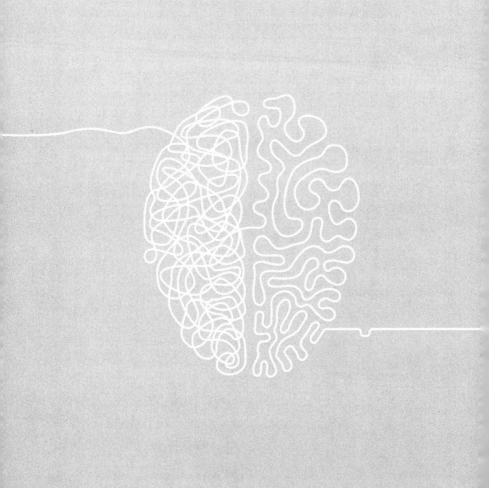

*9*

PRACTICE 6:
# Cultivate Certainty

Worry does not empty tomorrow of its sorrow.
It empties today of its strength.

**CORRIE TEN BOOM**

*Big idea:* Boost your tolerance to uncertainty to increase your
tolerance to stress.

*Bible insight:* God provides our ultimate source of certainty.

*Brain insight:* Uncertainty engages our brains' stress circuits.

*Best practice:* Surrendering prayer.

grew up afraid of the dark.

When my parents turned off the lights at night and we'd go to bed, I
covered my head with my blanket if I heard the faintest creak come from
our wooden floors. I'd think, "Did the bogeyman or a night monster make
that sound?" I gave my blanket a force field power to protect me from
anything nefarious.

My bedroom door was only five feet from the basement door, which
amplified my fear. Every kid knows where such creatures live: in the

*basement* (or under your bed if your house doesn't have a basement). When I heard any unexpected sound, my brain interpreted it as uncertainty and a threat to my safety, which ignited my brain's fear centers.

I grew out of my fear of the dark. At age thirty-four.

When we lived in Georgia I made a home office in the finished part of our basement. The other part of the basement, however, was unfinished and very, very dark. Unfamiliar sounds from the dark part evoked flashbacks to the monsters that lived in the dark part of our basement at my childhood home. I knew that at age thirty-four I must conquer my fear of the dark. After all, what if the church people I led at the time discovered that their pastor believed in imaginary creatures that lived in the dark part of his basement?

So, every day for weeks I crept into the foreboding part of the basement. As I inched deeper into the dark part, my heart raced and my hair stood on end. Fortunately, I never got attacked by a monster and no bogeyman ever hurt me. I convinced myself that such monsters never existed (or at least didn't live in my current basement).

I'm not afraid of the dark anymore, mostly.

Why did darkness scare me? It relates to how God wired our brains to respond to uncertainty and potentially harmful circumstances stemming from it. I had convinced myself that a monster lived in my basement. Although I had never seen it and the evidence didn't support its existence, something in my brain told me it existed and wanted to harm me. Although I imagined the threat, my brain registered it as real and it felt the same as if an actual threat existed. Uncertainty had triggered my brain's fear centers, and I sought safety beneath my imaginary force field blanket.

You may not fear the dark, but we all face uncertainty in various degrees, and it amplifies the negative effects from stress. Three thinking patterns can fuel the harmful effects from uncertainty: when we require exhaustive information during ambiguous experiences; when we assume the worst will happen; and when we lack confidence that we can make right choices in the future.[1] Although we can't control our uncertainty and the future, we can learn to become more tolerant of it and avoid the stress it creates.

This chapter, Practice 6: Cultivate Certainty, explains how we do that. You'll learn how the brain instigates and processes uncertainty and what Scripture says about it. You'll also discover a powerful practice that can minimize uncertainty-created stress. Dr. Kelly McGonigal found in her research that when we learn to tolerate uncertainty, we even view stress in a more positive way.[2]

## Bible Insight on Uncertainty

Unchecked uncertainty leads to worry and its cousins, rumination, anxiety, and fear. These emotional responses to uncertainty ignite the brain's stress response. Because Christians aren't immune to worry or its cousins, Jesus taught much about it (Matt. 6). One author wrote, "Christian worry is the unsuccessful human attempt, through cognitive and behavioral efforts, to obtain certainty about an ambiguous future because of the struggle to believe in, trust, and submit to the benevolent care of an omnipotent God."[3]

This secular definition of worry broadens the above definition and fits well within a biblical view.

Worry, at its core, is the repetitious experience of a mind attempting to generate a feeling of security about the future, failing, then trying again and again and again—as if the very effort of worrying might somehow help forestall disaster. The fuel behind worry, in other words, is the internal demand to know, in advance, that things will turn out fine. . . . But the struggle for control over the future is a stark example of our refusal to acknowledge our built-in limitations when it comes to time, because it's a fight the worrier obviously won't win. You can never be truly certain about the future. And so, your reach will always exceed your grasp.[4]

Worry can even become a tool we think can control the future and give us certainty. Worriers can link their worrying to a positive outcome. They worry that something bad may happen. It doesn't. So they conclude that their worry influenced the outcome. The bad thing didn't happen. They attribute their worry to an ability to keep bad things at bay. They surmise that worry must work and so they continue to worry and assume that it protects them. However, neither Scripture nor science supports that view.

What does Scripture say about uncertainty? It tells us that God gives us certainty because He Himself is our only true Certainty in an uncertain world. We don't know what tomorrow holds but we know who holds tomorrow. We can trust Him to give us a sense of certainty when life itself is uncertain.

The writer of Hebrews wrote, "Now faith is confidence in what we hope for and assurance about what we do not see" (Heb. 11:1). God's promises are certain because God does not lie (Num. 23:19). His promises are certain because of Jesus. "For no matter how many promises God has made, they are 'Yes' in Christ" (2 Cor. 1:20). The Bible illustrates God's faithfulness and dependability with several metaphors. He is our rock (Ps. 18:2), our foundation (1 Cor. 3:11), a tower we can run to (Prov. 18:10).

Matthew dedicates a significant portion in the Sermon on the Mount to Jesus' teaching on worry. Jesus said that birds and flowers don't sow, reap, labor, or spin because our heavenly Father provides for them. Yet we worry, "to increase certainty and control about future events, something Jesus instructed his audience not to do."[5] Jesus reminds us that although we live in an uncertain world, we can trust our heavenly Father to meet our needs. Faith in Him gives us certainty.

Researchers have discovered that when we sense a loss of control and turn to God, we regain a sense of control and certainty. They call it "compensatory control."[6] Compensatory control means that when we lack control in a circumstance, we turn to something or someone (God) we believe can control our circumstance. Scripture tells us that God controls the universe. "It is the LORD's purpose that prevails" (Prov. 19:21). "And we know that in all things God works for the good of those who love him, who have been called according to his purpose" (Rom. 8:28).

Compensatory control requires two fundamental beliefs. First, we must believe that God is benevolent and cares for us. Second, we must believe that He is competent enough to meet our needs.[7] Scripture tells us that God embodies both those qualities, and much more. His everlasting love for us reflects His benevolent love (Jer. 31:3). His omnipotence reminds us He is more than competent to meet our needs because all things are possible with God (Matt. 19:26).

In *My Utmost for His Highest*, Oswald Chambers describes how to respond to uncertainty.

> GRACIOUS UNCERTAINTY: " . . . it has not yet been revealed what we shall be. . . . " (1 Jn 3: 2). Our natural inclination is to be so precise—trying always to forecast accurately what will happen next—that we look upon uncertainty as a bad thing. We think that we must reach some predetermined goal, but that is not the nature of the spiritual life. The nature of the spiritual life is that we are certain in our uncertainty. . . . Certainty is the mark of the commonsense life—gracious uncertainty is the mark of the spiritual life. To be certain of God means that we are uncertain in all our ways, not knowing what tomorrow may bring. This is generally expressed with a sigh of sadness, but it should be an expression of breathless expectation. We are uncertain of the next step, but we are certain of God. . . . We are not uncertain of God, just uncertain of what He is going to do next. . . . Leave everything to Him and it will be gloriously and graciously uncertain how He will come in—but you can be certain that He will come. Remain faithful to Him.[8]

# Brain Insight on Uncertainty

Uncertainty evokes activity in several parts of our brains.[9] Pre-frontal cortex activity (the area behind your forehead involved in complex cognitive functions) shows a higher tolerance for uncertainty. The amygdala, involved in the fear response, engages during uncertainty. And higher levels of the neurotransmitter that regulates anxiety, GABA, helps the brain better tolerate ambiguity.

The brain is lazy and seeks to minimize how much energy it expends. That's why it prefers habits and outcomes that it can predict (certainty). Uncertainty requires more energy and hogs our cognitive resources.[10] If the uncertainty remains unresolved or we don't create a sense of certainty in the uncertainty, chronic stress can result and affect our brains and behavior in several ways.

- We catastrophize and create worst-case scenarios in our mind.[11]
- We delay decisions.[12]
- Dopamine, the feel-good neurotransmitter that aids memory and learning, decreases.[13]
- We get more easily distracted.[14]
- Our productivity decreases.[15]
- We become worse at affective forecasting, a term that describes how we think future events will affect us.[16] Uncertainty causes us to overestimate the intensity, harmfulness, and duration of a potentially stressful event. We then assume the future event will be worse than reality dictates. We underestimate our ability to weather it and ignore other events and values that could help us. Thus, it skews our ability to forecast how these events will affect us.
- It becomes rocket fuel for worry because we become hypervigilant and we "respond to threatening, stressful, or uncertain

circumstances with an outsized emotional response. [We] see threat everywhere. In fact, some people would rather accept a worse outcome in exchange for uncertainty's removal."[17]

Some people need more certainty than others because of genetic and personality differences. I'm an introvert and struggle with anxiety often caused by uncertainty. Uncertainty sometimes adds fuel to our anxiety.[18] Also, people who struggle with self-esteem need more certainty than others to quiet their brains' anxiety centers.[19] If you're an introvert or sometimes struggle with your self-concept, the best practice below will encourage you.

## Best Practice: Surrendering Prayer

Scripture often teaches that a healthy spiritual life includes prayer. Research has discovered that prayer can reduce intolerance to uncertainty,[20] decrease stress,[21] and minimize burnout.[22]

In an extensive study of more than 4,800 people, "All types of prayer predicted lower later stress and stress predicted lower later prayer."[23] Prayer also helps heal "the underlying emotional roots of stress."[24] This research, combined with compensatory control (see above) and the collaborative problem-solving style[25] revealed a type of prayer that can build our stress resilience during uncertainty. It's called surrendering prayer.

Surrendering prayer releases us from inner turmoil and stress as we become more aware of God's presence. Our goal in surrendering prayer is not simply to reduce stress, but to deepen our relationship with Jesus. Reduced stress in uncertainty becomes a by-product. Our emotional pain lessens and we can detach ourselves from the expectations and demands of others. We begin "to accept situations as they are, rather than what [we] think they should be."[26]

This idea finds its roots from the Jesuit priest Claude de la Colombière (1641–82). He taught that Christians can deal with the stressful experiences in life by surrendering to God.[27] This statement below summarizes how he defined surrendering prayer. Surrendering prayer is

> cultivating an awareness of God's attributes/actions—sovereignty, active presence, infinite wisdom, and benevolence. . . . [It] may help Christians to surrender to God's will during times of distress, and, thus, increase peace, happiness, and contentment. Strategies recommended to surrender to God's providential care include (a) practicing submission to God's will in smaller, day-to-day activities; and (b) placing faith and hope in God's protective care.[28]

For surrendering prayer to decrease uncertainty-prompted worry, we must embody three attitudes.[29] We must trust God's infinite wisdom in the uncertainty. We must believe that God always acts for our good. And we must believe that God is in total control.

One research study found that as we relinquish our own wills during uncertainty, we make room

> for God's intentions. . . . [We can] ameliorate worry because letting go, in and of itself, might cultivate a sense of well-being in that the cognitive exercise of worry is handed over to God. The ability to tolerate uncertainty helps this letting-go. Trusting in God's care may lead to a willingness to surrender that in turn may develop the skill of tolerating uncertainty because the future is in God's hands. So, when we have deep affective mental representations of God as caring and loving, we can tolerate uncertainty because God is in control of future events, is entirely fair as he orchestrates future events which leads to peace and well-being.[30]

Surrendering prayer, then, places our uncertain future in God's hands rather than our pursuing some pseudo-attempt to gain certainty.

In the above study, the researchers found positive effects in study participants who practiced prayer for as short a time as two weeks. They found that when we surrender, we allow God to change our perspective of the situation, rather than our trying to change the situation. We must set our goal, then, to "lean on God as a source of strength and guidance during difficult life events . . . [as we turn our] attention to God for strength, encouragement, protection, and comfort."[31]

Surrendering prayer helps us reduce stress as we reappraise uncertain situations. It helps us view our uncertainty through God's eyes rather than through our own skewed perspective.[32] We also shift to a more collaborative style of problem solving (see chapter 8 on collaborative problem solving).

Below I've listed the top ten benefits from surrendering prayer. Surrendering prayer helps us

1. settle our minds and hearts in uncertain situations.

2. re-perceive uncertainty as we accept situations as they are rather than what we think they should be.

3. increase our confidence that God can and will provide.

4. accept uncertainty as inevitable while we acknowledge God's sovereignty.

5. become present in the moment, which minimizes catastrophizing about the future.

6. create more pleasant affect through God-focused certainty since we often can't reduce exposure to uncertainty.[33]

7. create greater awareness of our negative responses to uncertainty so that we can yield them to God.

8. decrease activity in our brain's fear centers and boost activity in our thinking centers to expand our ability to cope with uncertainty.

9. lower our blood pressure and heart rate as it evokes the relaxation response.[34]

10. detach from the uncertain expectations and demands of others.

When you use surrendering prayer in an uncertain situation, keep in mind these three guidelines.[35] Admit that your circumstance lies outside your control. Affirm God's sufficiency. Relinquish your need to know.

Your prayer might be as simple as this, "Lord, You know I'm now in a difficult, uncertain spot [name the situation]. I affirm You love me, that You are in control of this situation, and that You will sustain me through it. I yield my thoughts, emotions, and actions in this circumstance to You. I surrender my need to know how things will turn out. Amen."

You can boost the effects of surrendering prayer if you journal your prayer.[36] However, don't let prayer work against you. Research shows that although prayer provides a powerful antidote to stress, it can increase anxiety if we focus too much on the circumstance. If your prayer entices you to ruminate and worry, focus less on the circumstance and more on God.[37]

In this chapter, Practice 6: Cultivate Certainty, you've learned how uncertainty affects us and a key spiritual best practice that helps us cope with it, surrendering prayer. The next chapter, Practice 7: Grow Gratitude, will unpack the power and beauty of a grateful heart.

## REVIEW

*Big idea:* Boost your tolerance to uncertainty to increase your tolerance to stress.

*Bible insight:* God provides our ultimate source of certainty.

*Brain insight:* Uncertainty quickly engages our brains' stress circuits.

*Best practice:* Surrendering prayer.

## APPLICATION

1. Reflect over the story about my fear of the dark. As a child did you have a similar fear? How do you think it affected your stress level?

2. This chapter listed three thinking patterns that fuel the harmful effects from uncertainty: requiring exhaustive information, assuming the worst, and lacking confidence in future choices. Which of these are sometimes true of you? How do they affect your stress resilience in uncertainty?

3. After reading the chapter, what brain or Bible insight did you most resonate with? Why? How might you apply it when you face uncertain circumstances that cause stress?

4. Reflect over an uncertain, stressful situation. If it happened again, how might you use surrendering prayer?

5. The chapter closed with the top ten benefits from surrendering prayer. What two benefits appealed to you the most? Why? How might you incorporate surrendering prayer into your daily routine to experience these benefits more often?

Continue to add to your Stress Resilience Plan.

For downloadable tools, visit this web link: www.charlesstone.com/stress.

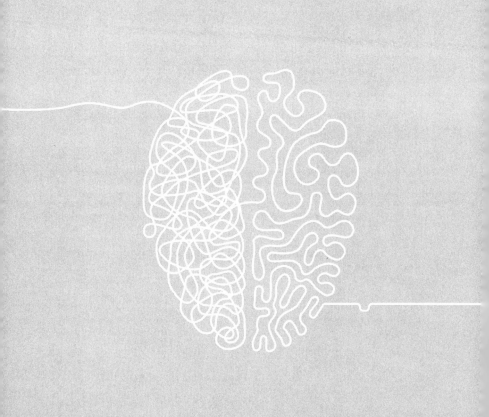

## PRACTICE 7:
# Grow Gratitude

*If life were a pizza, gratitude is its topping.*

**DR. AMIT SOOD**[1]

None is more impoverished than the one who has no gratitude. Gratitude is a currency that we can mint for ourselves, and spend without fear of bankruptcy.

**FRED DE WITT VAN AMBURGH**
*(1866–1944)*

*Big idea:* Grow your gratitude to stifle your stress.

*Bible insight:* Gratitude matters to God.

*Brain insight:* Gratefulness promotes brain health.

*Best practice:* Three Good Things.

met my wife-to-be at the Buddy's Winn-Dixie grocery store on Seminary Drive in Fort Worth, Texas. We both had enrolled in Southwestern Seminary and classes would begin soon. We didn't know each other yet, but we happened to shop for groceries at the same time in the same place.

As I pushed my buggy down the main aisle, I looked left and I saw this gorgeous girl (my future wife) standing in the aisle where the canned vegetables lined the shelves. A magnetic force drew my buggy to hers until they touched.

Sparks flew. I was goo-goo eyed.

We talked. I fell in love on the spot.

She didn't.

I asked for her address. She gave me the wrong one. To this day she claims that was not intentional.

I had fallen in love with Sherryl in 2.7 seconds. It took her 2.7 years to reciprocate.

As we developed our relationship prior to marriage, I visited her parents' home in Laurel, Mississippi. On that first visit her mother began to annoy me with constant "thank-yous" for everything I did.

I could take a fork off the kitchen table and put it in the dishwasher. Her mother would say with a Southern drawl, "Thank ya Chaaaarles!" I could bring napkins to the table for lunch and she'd say, "Thank ya Chaaaarles!" I could pick up a tiny speck of paper off the floor and put it into the garbage can and she'd say, "Thank ya Chaaaarles!" This constant barrage of "thank-yous" for everything I did chafed me.

My perspective on this irritation, however, changed. I could see that her thank-yous for small (and large) acts of service reflected genuine gratefulness. Over the years, I also noticed how her gratitude modeled this quality for Sherryl and her sister. To this day, Sherryl and her sister thank me for even the smallest things. That example spurred me to become more grateful as well. As I've practiced this trait, I've learned that gratitude builds resilience to stress, pleases God, and blesses others. This chapter unpacks this important quality.

## Bible Insight on Gratitude

Gratitude matters to God. Words like *gratefulness, thanksgiving,* and *gratitude* appear more than one hundred times in the Scriptures. Well-known verses include these (italics added):

"Give *thanks* in all circumstances; for this is God's will for you in Christ Jesus" (1 Thess. 5:18).

"Give *thanks* to the Lord, for he is good; his love endures forever" (Ps. 107:1).

"Enter his gates with *thanksgiving* and his courts with praise; give *thanks* to him and praise his name" (Ps. 100:4).

"Always [give] *thanks* to God the Father for everything, in the name of our Lord Jesus Christ" (Eph. 5:20).

"Let the message of Christ dwell among you richly as you teach and admonish one another with all wisdom through psalms, hymns, and songs from the Spirit, singing to God with *gratitude* in your hearts" (Col. 3:16).

"Do not be anxious about anything, but in every situation, by prayer and petition, with *thanksgiving*, present your requests to God" (Phil. 4:6).

Perhaps the greatest biblical example that illustrates how God values gratitude comes from an account Luke recorded when ten lepers confronted Jesus (Luke 17:11–19).

Leprosy attacks the body's nervous system and destroys pain receptors. As a result, lepers can inadvertently injure their body because pain no longer warns them to stop a damaging activity. Leprosy also grows ugly sores and tumors on the body. With no cure in biblical times, the disease brought stigma and disgrace to those afflicted with it. The populace believed that leprosy showed that God was displeased with the person. As a result, lepers' families and the village community would reject them. Fellow lepers became their only community.

Somehow this group of ten lepers had heard that Jesus had healed people. So, as He walked by them one day, they appealed to Jesus to heal them. On the spot He healed all ten. He told them to show themselves to the priests. His command related to a ritual whereby a priest could deem a leper clean so that he could re-enter society. Sometimes leprosy would go into remission and a priest would confirm that.

You can imagine the joy these lepers felt as they saw their tumors disappear and nubs grow into healthy fingers. All ten immediately sprinted to the village to find a priest. None of them thanked Jesus, with one exception.

That leper initially got caught up with the group's excitement as they all ran to town. Something, however, gave him pause. He realized that now his life would change forever for the good. Gripped with gratitude, he turned around and ran back to Jesus, maybe on new toes. Luke captures the leper's joy and gratitude with these words. "One of them, when he saw he was healed, came back, praising God in a loud voice. He threw himself at Jesus' feet and thanked him" (Luke 17:15–16).

Luke notes an irony, though. The leper who returned was a Samaritan, considered an outsider by the Jews. As the healed leper returned, Jesus expressed His disappointment that the other nine didn't. However, Jesus also affirmed the leper's gratitude when He said, "Rise and go; your faith has made you well" (Luke 17:19). The healed leper's gratefulness showed a changed heart. Not only did the grateful Samaritan receive a renewed body, but he received spiritual and emotional healing as well.

This story illustrates that God not only values gratitude, but that gratitude brings practical benefits to us as well. So, how does gratitude benefit our bodies and brains, and how might we develop it? The answer follows.

## Brain Insight on Gratitude

The research-based and highly acclaimed resilience training course developed at the Mayo Clinic by Dr. Amit Sood includes gratitude practice as a key pillar necessary to build resilience.[2] The course, called SMART, stands for Stress Management and Resiliency Training. Multiple studies on this course and its effects show that gratitude provides a powerful antidote to stress. Other studies have found that a grateful mindset leads to more positive emotions, less perceived stress, better health, and improved overall well-being.[3] My PhD research also supports this finding.

Gratitude engages several parts of our brains. It involves the brain's conductor (pre-frontal cortex), where high-level functions like emotional regulation, attention, and goal setting occur. It dampens the amygdala, the brain's primary fear center. And it engages the hippocampus, the brain's memory hub.

As gratitude affects these brain parts, they spur production of our feel-good neurotransmitters: dopamine, serotonin, and oxytocin. Gratitude activates both the parasympathetic nervous system (the calming system) and the dopamine system.[4] Dopamine connects positive behavior to pleasant emotions. When we practice gratitude and it feels good, we become more like likely to repeat it. Gratitude perpetuates itself.

When the parasympathetic nervous system gets activated, then activity in the sympathetic nervous system, responsible for our fight-or-flight response, decreases. Thus, it calms the amygdala, which reduces fear and reactive responses to stress.

Gratitude influences another part of the brain to increase the neurotransmitter serotonin.[5] Serotonin makes us feel good, helps us regulate emotions better, and helps us sleep better.[6]

Finally, gratitude spurs another part of the brain to release more oxytocin, the "cuddle hormone."[7] When we express gratitude to another person, the rise in oxytocin increases trust and helps us perceive love from each other better. We feel safe around that person and it encourages us to show more empathy,[8] all qualities that strengthen relationships. It also enhances future positive behaviors in relationships, called "pro-social behavior."[9]

Other benefits include these. Gratitude inhibits the brain from releasing the stress hormone, cortisol.[10] It decreases ongoing inflammation, which research ties to serious disease like diabetes, heart disease, and Alzheimer's.[11] It reduces depressive symptoms,[12] lowers blood pressure,[13] enhances recovery in health-related heart issues,[14] and strengthens our immune system.[15] Gratefulness even strengthens our attention so that we become more intentional about what we give our attention to.[16] What we pay attention to affects our thinking and emotions.

Lasting effects from gratefulness practices occur later as the benefits accrue. Neuroplasticity, the ability God gave our brain to change itself, doesn't happen overnight.[17] Don't expect that being grateful one day will boost long-term resilience. Make gratitude a habit so that it becomes second nature. Don't fix your mind on negative events.

Unfortunately, we pay more attention to negative events because the effects from the fall resulted in something called the "negativity bias." It takes time to counter that bias. However, "although the effects of bad [our innate tendency to notice it first] may be stronger, the effects of good may be longer . . . there may be a cumulative effect or a delayed effect for positive events."[18]

Like a conductor who coordinates all the instruments in a symphony to create a beautiful experience for the listener, gratitude does the same thing in our brain. It helps the brain's conductor (the pre-frontal cortex) synchronize brain chemicals and complex networks that influence memory, emotions, and reward. These cascade into a pleasant experience that benefits us in multiple ways. Most important, it brings joy to God's heart (see John 15:9–11; Prov. 17:11).

## Best Practice: Three Good Things

Gratitude grows our stress resilience best when we view it as a biblically rooted spiritual discipline we do each day.[19] The best practice for this practice, Grow Gratitude, requires a daily commitment called Three Good Things.

Three Good Things means to reflect on and even record three good things you've experienced or received after you get up and before you go to bed. This practice helps us remember, recall, and savor pleasant experiences that God gives us. Since we pay more attention to the negative than the positive, we need tools that help us recall the positive. Research says that when we record and reflect over our positive experiences,[20] we pay more attention to them, which decreases our stress.[21]

One study found that when participants recorded three good things each morning and why they considered them good, they experienced less stress in the afternoon. Positive morning events reduced afternoon stress. The researchers proposed four reasons to explain why this happened.[22]

First, when we record good things, it works against our bias to remember and expect the worst (the negativity bias). Second, it can counter our tendency to become accustomed to our circumstances and fail to notice the positive, called hedonic adaptation. Third, when we write about a positive experience it can help us relive the experience. This makes the event more accessible in memory, which increases the likelihood that we share our experience with another. And fourth, when we highlight what caused the positive event, it makes us more aware of resources available in our context to help us deal with the challenge.

Consider these practical ways to build Three Good Things into your routines.

*Buy a diary and record your three good things in it each morning and evening.* Positive journaling reduces stress.[23] As you record and think about these good things, your thinking will help you become more thankful. The philosopher Heidegger pointed out that "think" and "thank" share a common heritage. He taught that a "thinking that is thanking" was the best way to think.[24]

*Lower the threshold for what makes you grateful.* Don't simply seek grandiose reasons to experience gratefulness. Look for small, everyday experiences and blessings—like an unexpected act of kindness from a co-worker, your kids cleaning up their room without your asking, and noticing the first flower bloom in the spring. Make gratitude a daily disposition. Research shows that dispositional gratefulness boosts overall well-being.[25]

Dr. Amit Sood, one of the world's leading voices on stress resilience, told a story that illustrates someone with a low threshold for gratitude. Students and teachers alike called a little girl from an impoverished country the happiest kid in the school. Dr. Sood asked her what made her happy. She said, "I am happy because the grass is so green and soft." He asked what else. She replied, "The swing sets work, and the sky is so blue."[26] Her threshold for gratitude was low. Her happiness was high. Dr. Sood advises us, "Notice and savor the ordinary."[27]

*Use a gratitude jar at family meals.* Place a jar on your kitchen table along with a small pad of paper and a pen. Ask each family member to write out their Three Good Things and put them in the jar. Do this for a few days. Then, for a few days, take one list out at each family meal and read and discuss it. You may find interesting gratefulness themes in your family. Repeat the process when the lists in the jar run out.

*Write a gratitude letter to someone in your life you want to thank.* Even if you don't send it, research says it will boost your mental health and resilience.[28] Writing what we thank God and others for shifts our natural tendency from negative thinking to positive thinking.

*Map your gratefulness.*[29] On a piece of paper, write as many words as you can that describe what makes you grateful. Draw a circle around each. Then draw a line to another circle you create on the page. Within this circle write why the item you recorded in the first circle made you grateful. For example, you might write "my apartment" in the first circle. Then in the second circle you might write, "It feels like home." After you create your gratefulness map, thank God for each item. Post this "map" in a visible place in your home to remind you to prioritize gratefulness every day.

*Practice grounded optimism.* Grounded optimism means that we acknowledge a difficult situation, refuse to offer spiritual platitudes, and choose to act with gratefulness even if we don't feel like it. One study of Vietnam War prisoners found that reality-based optimism most strongly predicted their psychological health.[30]

A concept called the Stockdale Paradox came from this study. Researchers named it after admiral Jim Stockdale. He endured torture more than twenty times as a United States military officer held captive in North Vietnam for eight years. Nothing gave him reasons to believe he would survive imprisonment and see his wife again. And yet he never lost faith during his ordeal. He remained optimistic.

The paradox lies in Stockdale's optimism in face of the unknowable contrasted with the more optimistic prison mates who failed to survive. The pure optimists didn't face reality. They might still be in prison by the next Christmas, even though they optimistically proclaimed they'd be free by then. They preferred the ostrich approach, when we stick our heads in the sand and hope a difficulty goes away.

Their self-delusion might have made it easier on them in the short-term. However, when they faced reality (they didn't get out by Christmas), their mental state collapsed, they gave up, and they died. Gratitude doesn't imply that we ignore life's hardships. Rather, it means that in those circumstances we acknowledge reality, yet still choose gratefulness. Gratitude will increase optimism, which will build resilience.[31]

As we practice gratitude each day, we can move to deeper levels and enjoy more of its benefits. Dr. Sood classifies gratitude into these five levels.[32] Ask yourself what level describes your gratitude level. Aspire to move to the next higher one.

Level 1: Some people never experience gratitude. Nothing can please them.

Level 2: Some people experience gratitude when something extraordinary happens to them, like getting an unexpected tax refund.

Level 3: Some people experience gratitude when they enjoy life's daily pleasures, like a cup of hot coffee.

Level 4: Some people experience gratitude as a way of life. They need nothing external to experience it.

Level 5: Some people experience gratitude even in adversity. The apostle Paul reached this level. We see this disposition when he wrote about his trials (Rom. 5; 2 Cor. 11).

This chapter on gratitude unpacked the biblical and research basis to grow that character trait. A simple practice, Three Good Things, will deepen your resilience and bring joy to God and to others. The next chapter deals with a concept called psychological safety, how safe we feel around others.

### REVIEW

*Big idea:* Grow your gratitude to stifle your stress.

*Bible insight:* Gratitude matters to God.

*Brain insight:* Gratefulness promotes brain health.

*Best practice:* Three Good Things.

## APPLICATION

1. Recall a moment from last week when you expressed gratitude to someone. What did the person do or say in response? To whom could you express gratitude today?

2. Record your Three Good Things in the morning and before you go to bed. Review them when you get up. After a few days glean lessons, insights, or trends from your entries.

3. Choose one verse listed in this chapter (or pick your own). Spend five minutes reflecting over, personalizing, and praying through the verse. Record what resonates most. Why did it resonate with you? How might you build its truth deeper into your life today?

4. Recall a recent difficulty you faced. How could you have expressed gratitude in that situation and concurrently acknowledged reality?

5. Reread Dr. Sood's five gratitude levels. Pick the next highest one above the one you believe currently reflects your gratitude level. Write two steps you could take to move to that level and put on your calendar when you plan to take those steps.

Continue to add to your Stress Resilience Plan.

For downloadable tools, visit this web link: www.charlesstone.com/stress.

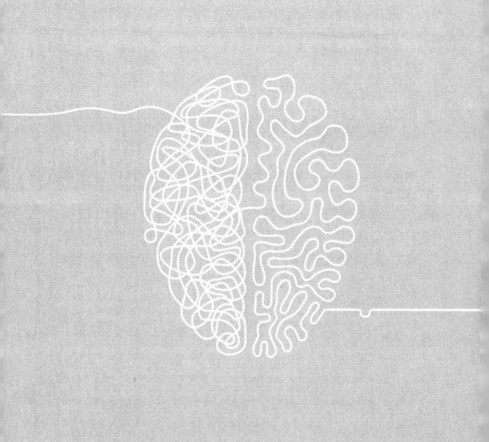

## PRACTICE 8:
# Safeguard Safety

A healthy relationship is one where
two independent people just make a deal
that they will help make the other person
the best version of themselves.

**UNKNOWN**

A real friend is one who walks in
when the rest of the world walks out.

**UNKNOWN**

*Big idea:* Develop and protect safe relationships to enhance your well-being and resilience.

*Bible insight:* Scripture values safe relationships within community.

*Brain insight:* When you don't feel safe around others, your brain's stress response activates.

*Best practice:* Build relationships with HEART.

My family lived in a Birmingham, Alabama, suburb when I entered the seventh grade. As a gangly twelve-year-old with bad acne, I lacked self-confidence. But I could run fast and I was smart. Those two qualities served me well that day in geography class.

I don't know what I did to irritate her. I don't know why she didn't like me. I don't know why she threatened me. But I'll never forget the day Helga (not her real name) sat behind me and told me something that affected me so much that I still remember it more than fifty years later.

Helga was twice my size.

Helga looked like a Viking.

Helga liked to be in control.

Ten minutes before the bell rang for class to end, she leaned over and whispered in my ear, "When class is over, I'm going to beat you up."

At that moment the hands on the aluminum-framed, square clock on the wall behind the teacher began to move in slow motion. Ten minutes seemed to stretch into sixty.

But, because I was smart and fast, I planned my response. I had ten minutes (or sixty, depending on how you looked at it). I slowly placed my books in my backpack, I slipped on my backpack without drawing the teacher's attention, I shifted my legs from under the desk into the aisle, and I took the sprinter's pose.

The clock rang for class to end.

Before the teacher could finish, "Class, have a good rest of the day," like Flash the superhero, my sprint out the door left a faint light trail. And before Helga knew what happened, I had taken shelter on the other side of the school.

I guess Helga got over it. She didn't threaten me after that day. She still looked like a Viking. But I made sure I didn't sit in front of her again. And I always sat close to the door, just in case.

Why did that incident affect me so much? It threatened two kinds of safety. First it threatened my physical safety, which we intuitively understand. If she smacked me with a left hook, it would hurt and maybe loosen some molars.

But it also threatened my psychological safety, a concept less understood, but powerful. If I had failed to elude her and she had beaten me up in front of others, I'd feel shame and disgrace before my classmates. My soul would experience a wound that would outlast any physical wound. The social hit from the embarrassment would last longer for me than if she had knocked out a few teeth. Psychological hits go deeper and last longer than physical hits.

My experience illustrates psychological safety, a buzzword prominent in the business community today. Dr. Amy Edmondson, Harvard School professor who authored the book *The Fearless Organization*, coined the phrase. Psychological safety means that we feel safe and secure around others. We can express our opinions, share ideas, and even make mistakes without fearing they will embarrass, punish, or reject us.[1]

In this chapter on the eighth practice, Safeguard Safety, you'll understand what safety, or lack thereof, does to your brain, what Scripture says about safe relationships, and a best practice that builds psychological safety.

## Bible Insight on Psychological Safety

We need safe people in our lives for our overall well-being and our spiritual and psychological health. Significant research reinforces that truth.[2] Although Scripture doesn't explicitly use the phrase *psychological safety*, the concept weaves its way throughout the Bible. It describes safety with God and with people.

The Old Testament describes God as a safe place (italics mine):

"You will be secure, because there is hope; you will look about you and take your rest in *safety*" (Job 11:18).

"In peace I will lie down and sleep, for you alone, LORD, make me dwell in *safety*" (Ps. 4:8).

"You, LORD, will keep the needy *safe* and will protect us forever from the wicked" (Ps. 12:7).

"Trust in the LORD and do good; dwell in the land and enjoy *safe* pasture" (Ps. 37:3).

"The name of the LORD is a fortified tower; the righteous run to it and are *safe*" (Prov. 18:10).

The New Testament describes the church as a community and sometimes uses the word *koinonia*, which means deep partnership. God made us to enjoy safe relationships while in community with Him and others. The Trinity pictures a perfect community. Well-being requires safe friends and relationships in a biblical community that embraces psychological safety (italics mine below).

"They devoted themselves to the apostles' teaching and to *fellowship*, to the breaking of bread and to prayer" (Acts 2:42).

"God is faithful, who has called you into *fellowship* with his Son, Jesus Christ our Lord" (1 Cor. 1:9).

In Philippians 1:3–11, the apostle Paul, writing as their pastor, described several key qualities we need while in community with safe friends.

A safe friend will remember the best about you (v. 3). When Paul prayed for his friends in the church in Philippi, his thoughts about them brought him great joy. He focused on their good qualities rather than on their limitations and weaknesses. He remembered their best.

Safe friends will give their best to you (vv. 5, 7). Paul wrote that he "had them in [his] heart." He fully gave himself to them when he gave them his heart. Paul didn't make surface relationships.

A safe friend will encourage the best in you (v. 6). He felt confident that God would finish the work that He had begun in them to bring out their best. Good friends will bring out your best. Author Liz

Wiseman, who studied 150 leaders for her book *Multipliers: How the Best Leaders Make Everyone Smarter,* discovered that leaders fall into two categories: multipliers and diminishers. Multipliers bring out the best in others because they amplify their strengths, encourage them, and empower them. Diminishers do the opposite. They drain others when they micromanage, convey they have all the answers, and act with a big ego. Safe friends, however, act as multipliers in our lives.

A safe friend will pray the best for you (v. 9). Paul fervently prayed for his friends. He prayed they would love Jesus and others more, would learn more about God, and would allow His Word to shape their conduct and character. Safe friends will pray for these three qualities to root themselves in their friends' characters.

Finally, a safe friend will expect the best from you (vv. 10–11). Safe friends will hold you accountable. They will tell you what you may not want to hear because they will expect the best from you. They will challenge you to do and be your best, but with grace.[3]

Several qualities the apostle Paul emphasized in the passage above support the best practice I explain later in this chapter.

## Brain Insight on Psychological Safety

Dr. Stephen Porges, creator of the Polyvagal Theory,[4] coined the term "neuroception" in 2004 to describe our brain's non-conscious process that assesses safety or threat cues. This "safety scanner" gathers information about our environment, our heart rate, our respiration, facial cues from others, and subtle shifts in tone of voice to determine safety or threat. He proposes that when we feel safe around others, a social engagement circuit engages to help us feel calm, reduce stress, decrease defensiveness, and become more open to others. And when we don't feel safe, two other brain circuits activate, which can cause chronic stress, anxiety, depression, and helplessness.

Without a healthy and safe social network, we increase our risk factor for death, equivalent to smoking fifteen cigarettes a day. Social isolation harms us even more than obesity, lack of exercise, or drinking too much alcohol does.[5] Social isolation can lead to chronic stress that stimulates growth in our fear center, the amygdala, and atrophies in our brain's thinking center, the pre-frontal cortex, which affects our mood and cognition.[6]

When we lack safe relationships or our relationships get strained, the language we use reminds us we feel stress. We use terms to describe emotional pain like having a "broken" heart or being "hurt" by another. Other languages use similar phrases.[7]

However, healthy, safe relationships can keep chronic stress in check. Stress expert Kelly McGonigal writes that stress can "activate pro-social instincts, encourage social connection, and enhance social cognition." As a result, we "want to be near [safe] friends or family . . . [and] feel a desire to protect, support, or defend the people . . . [we] care about."[8] God created in us an innate desire to seek safe relationships when we face stress.

For decades, research has found that healthy social relationships enhance our well-being. The Blue Zones study,[9] a recent example of such research, isolated geographical regions around the globe where the world's oldest people lived. The study found that good community, a common factor, contributed to their longevity. Neuroscientists Tabibnia and Radecki also found that "increasing feelings of belonging, companionship, self-esteem, and self-efficacy" enhanced overall well-being.[10]

Our brains work on autopilot most of the time.[11] The brain receives 11 million bits of information per second and it can only process about forty of them per second.[12] Fortunately, God automated our brains with unconscious mental shortcuts that help us manage much more.[13] This process, however, sometimes goes awry.

Early in the book I noted God wired our brains with a fundamental organizing principle: minimize danger/threat and maximize safety/

reward.[14] The massive daily data we receive can sometimes cause us to perceive a threat or lack of safety when one does not exist. When we don't feel safe around others, whether danger is real or imagined, the brain activates the stress response.[15]

Fortunately, God gave us executive functions that our brain's pre-frontal cortex executes when we don't feel safe. It helps us pay attention, control our emotions, think rationally about situations, see different perspectives, and empathize with others. It helps us sort out real versus imaginary threats to safety through a built-in braking system[16] that inhibits unhealthy responses and impulses. However, this thinking part of our brain requires substantial energy (oxygen and glucose). When it works in overdrive to inhibit unhealthy impulses, it can become fatigued and work less efficiently. That why we need regular daily rest breaks and good sleep (the next chapter) to recharge our brains.

Researchers have discovered that even a safe touch improves our well-being. "Caring physical contact from people we know and trust lowers our biological threat response, improves our ability to deal with stress, promotes relationship satisfaction, and reduces feelings of loneliness. It also activates the brain's reward circuitry and triggers the release of stress-relieving neurochemicals such as oxytocin and endorphins."[17]

Our brains love safe environments and safe people. So how can we experience safety more often?

## Best Practice to Build Psychological Safety

The best practice to help build safety is this: Build relationships with HEART. The letters in this acronym represent five qualities to seek in potential safe relationships and to model yourself. Building safety requires reciprocity. It's not a one-way street. We won't find a perfectly safe person and we won't be perfectly safe ourselves. However, as we build and share our HEART, we will connect with other people with HEART as well.

The five qualities follow, and a more detailed explanation follows that.

H: **h**appy

E: **e**mpathetic

A: **a**ware

R: **r**ealistic

T: **t**rustworthy

*Happy* in this context implies a positive disposition we show as a way of life. It doesn't mean we fake or force a smile. Sometimes we don't feel happy. It means that with God's power we try to experience both the abundant life Jesus promised and the fruit of the Spirit.

Jesus said, "I have come that they may have life, and have it to the full" (John 10:10). The apostle Paul wrote, "But the fruit of the Spirit is love, joy, peace, forbearance, kindness, goodness, faithfulness, gentleness and self-control. Against such things there is no law" (Gal. 5:22–23).

When we live out these happiness qualities, an interesting phenomenon occurs, as an extensive study of more than 4,700 people found. Researchers discovered that people who surround themselves with happy people are happier now and in the future.[18] It's called emotional contagion. Like a virus, we catch emotions from others, and they catch them from us, whether positive or negative ones. Even social media fosters emotional contagion. When we view more negative content on it, we post negative content and vice versa.[19]

So, if we want to find and build safe relationships, we must live a biblically happy lifestyle.

*Empathetic* means that we maintain our full presence with others in their pain and that they maintain their presence with us in ours. Safe people won't dismiss our pain, yet they will love us enough to not let our pain drown us. We can be ourselves around them and they with us.

Scripture tells us to bear one other's burdens and pain. Paul wrote,

"Carry each other's burdens" (Gal. 6:2). God wired us to desire that others validate our pain. When they do, it connects us to them, makes us feel like we belong, and releases the neurotransmitter oxytocin, which enhances safety.[20]

Building a safe relationship requires that we empathize, stand with others in their pain.

*Aware* means that we know the triggers that evoke threat. We know the buttons, when pushed, that engage our stress response. Although we could list many stressors that do that, a few common ones stand out: fear of embarrassment (remember Helga?), loss of control, performance pressure, anger directed at us, conflict, time pressure, financial stress, and saying yes when we shouldn't have. Past trauma may also trigger a threat.[21]

A safe person will know you well enough to avoid your triggers. It may take time to build that insight with each other, but it's time well spent.

*Realistic* means that a safe friend will keep us grounded. With love they will speak truth into our lives and we into theirs. The relationship strength gives permission to say hard things and not feel rejected or rebuffed. Neuroscientist Ethan Kross explains why we need both emotional presence and loving honesty:

> We tend to overfocus on our emotional needs to the detriment of finding solutions to our stressful situation. When we feel negative emotions and share it with a friend, we don't want to be sucked into further rumination of that hurt. We don't want one negative thought to breed another one and then more after that. It's important to combine both a mentality of Kirk in Star Trek, who was the emotional one, and Spock, who was the logical one. So, the kind of friend we need is one who will listen to our pain, but not egg it on. They should also help us think through what we need to do in response to our stress.[22]

*Trustworthy* includes several components.[23]

Integrity: Trust doesn't play favorites. It treats critics with respect. It never cuts moral corners.

Reciprocation: If we extend trust to others, they will give it back to us. If we don't trust others, don't expect them to trust us. Trust gets reciprocated. If we want trust, we must give trust.

Transparency: People don't trust what they don't see. Trust requires humility. And humility often means that we become vulnerable to others. When we do, we give others power to potentially hurt or disappoint us. Trust comes when we take such risks.

Excuse-making: Trust never makes excuses or tries to cover up. It owns its failures. Trust apologizes and makes restitution when necessary. It never blames others for its mistakes.

Follow through: trust follows through on what it says it will do. It's not all talk and no action.

Understanding: Trust seeks understanding before being understood. Trust listens.

Care: Earlier in the book I used a piggy bank to describe how we can put pleasure coins into a pleasure piggy bank. The metaphor also applies here. We can only deposit physical coins into a piggy bank one at a time. However, if we pull the plug from the piggy bank, those coins fall out all at once. A trust piggy bank acts in the same way. Although trust builds slowly, it can quickly disappear when it's broken.

So, we can safeguard safety when we build relationships with people with HEART and as we live as people with HEART.

The next chapter completes the nine practices with one crucial, often overlooked practice, Sleep Smart.

## REVIEW

*Big idea:* Develop and protect safe relationships to enhance your well-being and resilience.

*Bible insight:* Scripture values safe relationships within community.

*Brain insight:* When you don't feel safe around others, your brain's stress response activates.

*Best practice:* Build relationships with HEART.

## APPLICATION

1. Reflect on your current relationships. How well do you show the HEART qualities (Happy, Empathetic, Aware, Realistic, Trustworthy)? What one quality could you pick this week to improve?

2. List your top two or three personal triggers. What close friend or family member could you share those with to foster a more psychologically safe environment?

3. Consider your small group or Sunday school class. How might you introduce to your group the ideas in HEART that could deepen your fellowship?

4. Which Scripture in the chapter resonated with you the most and why?

5. Consider an experience when you felt psychologically unsafe. What made you feel that way? What could you have done differently to feel more psychologically safe?

Continue to add to your Stress Resilience Plan.

For downloadable tools, visit this web link: www.charlesstone.com/stress.

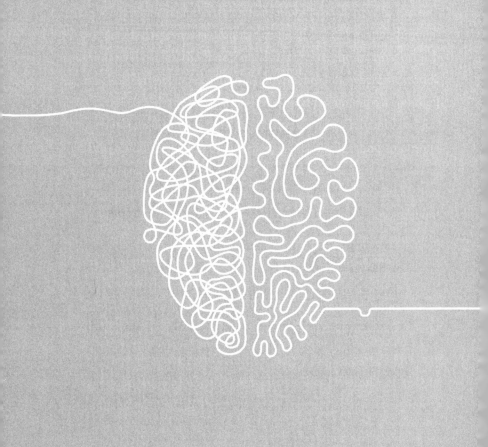

# PRACTICE 9:
# Sleep Smart

The worst thing in the world is to try to sleep and not to.

**F. SCOTT FITZGERALD**
*American author (1896–1940)*

*Big idea:* Prioritize healthy sleep habits to cushion the effects from chronic stress.

*Bible insight:* The Bible references sleep more than one hundred times.

*Brain insight:* Good sleep habits maximize the positive benefits from your brain's sleep chemicals.

*Best practice:* The Four-Stage Sleep Box Strategy.

'm a light sleeper. A refreshing night of sleep often eludes me. I've tried almost every trick to sleep better. I sleep so poorly that a surprising culprit once woke me up.

I joined a Christian fraternity in my last year at Georgia Tech and lived at the frat house. My small bed sat next to a shelf that held a few essential foods every college student needs: Cheerios, ramen noodles, and canned chili. One night while in a deep sleep I thought I had dreamed that I heard a sound like *pitter-patter, pitter-patter, pitter-patter*. Then it stopped. A few moments later I knew I wasn't dreaming when I heard another sound. This time it was *crunch, crunch, crunch.* My bleary eyes focused on my box of Cheerios on the shelf, and I saw the culprit. A tiny mouse had nibbled through the box and was enjoying a late-night snack.

This stinkin' mouse woke me up from a rare deep sleep. I guess he hadn't heard the adage, "Quiet as a mouse."

That experience illustrates my lifelong struggle to sleep well. I sleep better now because I've applied several science-based insights I describe below. The insights in this chapter, Practice 9: Sleep Smart, will show you how to experience consistent, healthy sleep. Healthy sleep makes our bodies and brains more resilient to stress. And whether you sleep poorly or sleep well, you'll find these insights helpful as you build your Stress Resilience Growth Plan.

This chapter includes four sections instead of the three-section pattern in the prior practice chapters. I first summarize the disturbing state of sleep in the world today. Second, you'll learn what Scripture says about sleep. Third, I'll explain neuroscience insights about sleep's benefits. Finally, you'll preview a tool called the Four-Stage Sleep Box. This tool visualizes evidence-based skills that can help you grow (or sustain) consistent, healthy sleep.

## The State of Sleep Today

Sleep is in trouble today. Many people sleep poorly, exacerbated by the effects from the Covid epidemic. Forty percent of Americans say they suffered from some sleep issue in the past twelve months.[1] Almost 20 percent of American adults use over the counter or prescription drugs to help them sleep,[2] even though research shows that these drugs only marginally improve sleep quality and length.[3] Sleep disorders cost the US almost 100 billion dollars a year.[4]

Research has linked poor sleep to hypertension, depression, dementia, diabetes, obesity, cancer, poor memory, negative mood, low moral awareness, and poor learning ability.[5] Chronic poor sleep impairs our driving skills as much as driving legally drunk.[6] Obstructive sleep apnea, a serious sleep issue, affects 30 million Americans. Many cases go undiagnosed.[7] Apnea occurs when we sleep and our throat's soft tissues relax and partially or fully close our airways, which decreases the oxygen our brains need. Overall, poor sleep affects how we think, how we feel, and our physical health.

Doctors receive little training in sleep. One study from Harvard found that a medical student's curriculum only included about two hours in sleep instruction.[8] And Americans aren't taking steps to sleep better, either.

Each year an organization conducts the Sleep in America poll. It analyzes how well Americans keep ten healthy sleep habits and gives a grade from A to F. The 2023 grades were dismal. Fifty-two percent got a D or an F. Only 26 percent got an A or a B. That is, only a quarter of Americans practice good sleep habits. The Four-Stage Sleep Box strategy, however, can lift or keep your grade in the A or B category. It gives you another tool for your stress resilience toolbox.

## Bible Insight on Sleep

The word *sleep* appears more than 125 times in the New International Version of the Bible. It could mean sex, physically sleeping with someone, or a metaphor for death. However, the biblical writers often use it to describe sleep itself.

Three biblical examples include these. God put Adam to sleep to take a rib to make Eve (Gen. 2:21). Jesus slept in a boat during a squall on the Sea of Galilee (Matt. 8:24). And the disciples slept while Jesus agonized in the garden of Gethsemane (Matt. 26:40).

Several other verses illustrate sleep-related themes. They include sleep in context of God's peace and safety, His rest to those He loves, and encouragement to cast our anxieties on Him to find true rest.

The psalmist reminds us that God wants us to sleep well (Ps. 4:8). He keeps us secure in His love as He watches over us when we sleep (Ps. 3:5). We depend on His care as we sleep. Jesus experienced this when He slept in a boat in a storm. Sleep reminds us about eternity and our mortality (1 Thess. 5:10).

Although the biblical writers didn't study sleep, their writings illustrate key sleep concepts. Sleep drive, also called sleep inertia, describes when sleep overwhelms our desires to stay awake and we fall asleep. The disciples illustrated sleep drive when Matthew wrote they couldn't stay awake for Jesus when they were in the garden of Gethsemane before His arrest (Matt. 26:40).

The psalmist may illustrate another scientific insight. Your mind doesn't shut down during sleep. During REM (rapid eye movement) sleep it repeats some information you learned during the prior day. So, when the psalmist wrote that the godly person meditates on God's Word "day and night" (Ps. 1:2), we should aspire to have it so deeply rooted that it is in our mind even when we sleep. Samuel hints at sleep stages (there are four) when he describes Saul and his men in a deep sleep (1 Sam. 26:12). Saul's deep sleep allowed David to take Saul's water jar and spear without waking him, which later reminded him that David could have taken his life.

The Bible also frowns upon undisciplined sleep patterns (Ps. 127:2) and oversleeping (Prov. 6:9). The apostle Paul even includes sleeplessness when he lists his trials and tribulations as he followed Jesus (2 Cor. 6:5). If you've ever experienced chronic insomnia, you can identify with Paul. Perpetual sleeplessness, insomnia, can feel like a trial.

Roman Catholic, Lutheran, Anglican, and Eastern Orthodox churches teach the office of compline, or night prayer, a spiritual discipline related to sleep.[9] This discipline includes prayers for peace and sound sleep. Theologian D. A. Carson writes this insight about sleeplessness, "Doubt may be fostered by sleep deprivation. . . . We are whole, complicated beings;

our physical existence is tied to our spiritual well-being, to our mental outlook, to our relationships with others, including our relationship with God. Sometimes the godliest thing you can do in the universe is get a good night's sleep."[10]

## Brain Insight on Sleep

Sleep benefits our bodies, brains, and relationships multiple ways and undergirds stress resilience. These word pictures illustrate these benefits.

- A bilge pump . . . Just as a bilge pump removes garbage, sleep does the same through a recently discovered system called the glymphatic system. When the neurons in our brain fire, they leave behind metabolic debris, including proteins implicated in Alzheimer's disease. God created our brains with a fluid, cerebrospinal fluid, that circulates in our brains and spinal cords. At night "helper" brain cells called glia shrink[11] to make it easier for the fluid to flow so it can take out the trash. So sleep protects our brains from harmful substances.

- A painter . . . Just as painters set their artwork aside for the paint to harden, sleep hardens the memories we want to keep. This process, consolidation,[12] moves important memories from shorter term memory to long-term memory. So sleep enhances memory.

- A librarian . . . After library hours a librarian will reshelve books left in disarray in the book returns. Librarians make order out of chaos when they put books back on the shelves in their proper places. Sleep acts in the same way. It takes the various disconnected thoughts from our day and makes order out of them, placing them where they need to go. It takes the raw material of thought, tidies it up, and helps form associations between seemingly unrelated thoughts.[13] Sleep makes order out of chaos.

- A builder . . . Just as a builder creates new things, sleep helps form new brain cells, a process called neurogenesis. This occurs primarily in the brain's chief memory processing center, the hippocampus. Although these baby neurons total only about one thousand per day,[14] every bit helps. Poor sleep hinders this process to enhance memory.[15]

- An editor . . . Editors remove unneeded words and sentences from books and articles. Likewise, our brains record our experiences and memories during the day and edit them at night. Sleep makes our brains switch to edit mode to edit memories we don't need. We forget what we need to forget.[16] Some forgetting is necessary or else our brains would grow to a size the skull could not contain. The massive information would explode our brains. So we sleep to remember and sleep to forget.[17]

- A counselor . . . A counselor helps us process difficult emotions and memories. Likewise, sleep down-regulates unpleasant emotions and helps us process the issues that fuel them.[18] This occurs because norepinephrine, the neurotransmitter that supercharges emotions, decreases during dream sleep.[19] So sleep helps us resolve emotional pain.

- A mechanic . . . A mechanic fixes car problems and tunes up engines to make them run smoother. Sleep acts like a mechanic because it fine-tunes our ability to read other people's emotions.[20] Healthy relationships depend on our ability to read emotions correctly. However, poor sleep increases the likelihood that we read fear from other people's facial expressions where none exists.[21] So sleep can enhance relationships.

Good sleep also helps in other ways. It improves impulse control,[22] the ability to say no to that second piece of chocolate cake. It helps us maintain a healthy weight because good sleep increases the hormone leptin, which tells us we are full. Poor sleep increases the hormone ghrelin, which makes us hungry. Good sleep also enhances immunity[23] so that we can stave off sickness and recover better when sick. Finally, sleep enhances creativity and problem solving because it fuses together disparate sets of information (the librarian above).[24] Neuroscience supports the adage "Sleep on it" to help us solve problems.

So, getting a good night's sleep benefits us in multiple ways.

## Best Practice: Four-Stage Sleep Box Strategy

Our brains engage about 50 percent of brain circuitry to process visual information.[25] That insight will help you better remember the Four-Stage Sleep Box strategy with the image below.

Four quadrants form the box, and each quadrant includes one image. Each image portrays one concept in the Sleep Box Strategy. Quadrant one visualizes a toothbrush, to represent sleep hygiene. Quadrant two, a car, represents sleep drive. Quadrant three, a clock, represents our body clock. And quadrant four, a megaphone, represents our alerting or awake system.[26]

Before I unpack the Four-Stage Sleep Box strategy, it's helpful to understand how sleep works in our brains, a cycle called sleep architecture. Earlier I noted that scientists have discovered that understanding how the brain works, like how it processes pain, helps build stress resilience.[27] It's called psycho-education. Research shows it helps us process psychological and physiological distress, including poor sleep.[28] When we understand how sleep works, we gain another helpful sleep tool. I include a brief primer on sleep below. The Sleep Box will build on this foundation.

First, the latest research tells us we need around seven hours of sleep each night,[29] not seven hours in bed, but seven hours asleep. We can't make up chronic sleep debt by sleeping in on weekends. However, we can slowly repay our sleep debt by getting a bit more sleep each night. It takes about four nights of good sleep to make up for one hour of sleep debt.[30] The brain compensates for lost sleep by increasing deep and dream sleep in subsequent nights.[31] Also, our body temperature drops 1.5 to 2 degrees at night to promote good sleep. Eating a big meal at night inhibits good sleep because our core temperature stays higher while it digests our food.

Sleep involves these three primary processes: sleep drive (also called system S or sleep pressure), the sleep clock (also called system C or our circadian rhythm), and the sleep arousal system (also called the alerting system).

## SLEEP DRIVE

Sleep drive and the neurotransmitter adenosine regulate how much sleep we need. Based on our daily activity and our awake time, it accumulates in our brain. The longer you stay awake, the more adenosine accumulates, and the sleepier you get. Our bodies' energy-producing process creates this neurotransmitter.

Adenosine is like air in a balloon. A full balloon exerts significant pressure. A partially filled one doesn't. Likewise, a brain full of adenosine will exert significant sleep pressure to make us sleepy. Low adenosine doesn't. Good daily habits keep adenosine at beneficial levels (more on that below). However, long naps and caffeine in the afternoon can make our adenosine balloon flabby.

## SLEEP CLOCK

Our sleep clock regulates sleep and wakefulness timing. It's called the circadian rhythm and acts like an internal biological clock. God designed us to live within a twenty-four-hour cycle. This cycle exceeds twenty-four hours by a few minutes, so we need daily cues to keep our clock on time. These cues, called zeitgebers (German for "time-cue"), manage this drift to keep our bodies on schedule. These cues include the daytime-nighttime cycle, a regular bedtime, and consistent mealtimes.

A tiny collection of brain cells (the suprachiasmatic nucleus) sits atop the intersection of our optic nerves and forms our sleep clock. It receives light information from our eyes. At night when it gets dark, it informs the pea-sized pineal gland to release the vampire sleep hormone, melatonin. It only comes out at night. Melatonin acts like the official at a track meet who raises a hand with a pistol and says, "On your mark. Set. Go!" (and fires the pistol). It tells our body it's time to go to sleep. When we wake up and sunlight enters our eyes, our sleep clock puts the brake pedal on the pineal gland to stop producing melatonin. By this time melatonin has already somewhat dissipated.

However, artificial light in the evening can trick our sleep clock to think it's still daytime, which suppresses melatonin. Blue light, which lies on the short end of the light spectrum, is especially disruptive because the light receptors in our eyes are more sensitive to it.[32] Significant blue light comes from our computer, TV, and handheld screens. You'll see below that good sleep hygiene includes limiting screen use an hour prior to bedtime.

## AWAKE SYSTEM

Our awake system, also called arousal or alertness, keeps us attentive during the day. Both our external environment and our internal thoughts and emotions influence this system. When it's not in a balanced state, we don't sleep well. Light, noise, and temperature in the environment can affect this system. False beliefs about sleep (e.g., "I *must* get eight hours of sleep") can affect it. Anxiety, worry, and a bad mood can also throw this system off.

Insomniacs struggle more from an impaired mood. Sleep loss reduces an important neurotransmitter involved in our brain's reward pathway, dopamine,[33] which decreases positive emotions. Poor sleep also fatigues our brain connections between our thinker (pre-frontal cortex) and our feeler (the amygdala), which keeps our emotions amped up and less able to control our emotion-fueled behavior.[34]

## SLEEP STAGES

God designed us to sleep in four stages. Light sleep is called N1 and N2. Deeper sleep is called N3 and REM (rapid eye movement) sleep. We usually move through four to six ninety-minute cycles each night. During light sleep (N1/N2), several synchronized activities overlap. N3 is called slow wave sleep, or deep sleep, when our oxygen consumption and heart rate fall to their lowest evening levels. This stage restores our body and brain more than the other stages. During REM sleep we experience our most vivid dreams. In this stage, our brains paralyze our bodies (this is called atonia) so that we don't act out our dreams. However, those with parasomnia sleep disorders can bypass this paralyzed state, which causes disorders like sleepwalking or sleep terrors.

Most of our non-REM deep sleep occurs in the first half of the night, and most of our REM sleep occurs in the last half. Babies and children need more sleep than adults. And as we age, we need less sleep, but no less than seven hours. Unfortunately, as we age, we get less deep sleep.

## THE FOUR-STAGE SLEEP BOX STRATEGY EXPLAINED

The Sleep Box strategy includes practical ways to enhance your sleep whether or not you sleep well. If given an opportunity to sleep, a sleep-deprived person could sleep. However, someone who suffers from chronic insomnia, if given the opportunity to sleep, can't sleep well. Chronic insomnia results in poor daytime mood like irritability, fatigue, and reduced motivation, but not always decreased productivity. If you consistently don't sleep well, you may suffer from clinical insomnia. The criterion for insomnia is sleep disruption at least three times a week for three months with negative effects on daily life.

The American College of Physicians recommends cognitive-behavioral therapy for insomnia (CBT-I) as a first choice to treat insomnia.[35] Many times it works better than sleep medications. It's effective even if a person doesn't meet the criteria for chronic insomnia. If you think you may suffer from insomnia, consult a trained sleep coach or counselor. You might also try online CBT-I software proven to treat insomnia successfully.[36]

Obstructive sleep apnea is a serious sleep issue that warrants medical help. We experience an apnea in our sleep if our air flow reduces by at least 90 percent for at least ten seconds. Both in-home and sleep clinic studies can confirm apnea. If you think you may suffer from apnea, use the STOPBANG questionnaire below to self-identify it.[37] If you check three or more you may have apnea. Consult your doctor in that case.

___ **S**noring: You snore at night.

___ **T**iredness: You experience daytime tiredness.

___ **O**bserved apnea: Someone has noticed your breathing stop at night.

___ **P**ressure: You have high blood pressure.

___ **B**MI: It's higher than 35.

___ **A**ge: You are 50 or older.

___ **N**eck circumference: It's greater than 16 inches.

___ **G**ender: You are male.

I explain the steps in the Sleep Box below and include specific steps in each quadrant. Don't apply them all at once. Pick one from each box to try this week and then gradually add more steps that apply to your situation.

## PRACTICE GOOD SLEEP HYGIENE

Just as good body hygiene promotes good physical health, good sleep hygiene promotes good sleep.

1. Create a good sleep environment. Use a good pillow and mattress. Keep your room cool at night (mid-sixties). Use light-blocking curtains if light seeps through your window shades in the morning. If noise disturbs your sleep, try ear plugs, sound blocking earbuds, or a white-noise machine.

2. Keep a consistent sleep schedule, even on weekends. Get up no later than thirty minutes after your alarm awakens you.

3. Avoid heavy meals three hours prior to bedtime. It's fine to eat a healthy snack before bedtime, but avoid spicy, fatty, or high-carb evening meals.

4. Don't drink alcohol at night. A so-called "night cap" may help you fall asleep quicker, but it will fragment your sleep, which results in poor sleep.

5. Don't exercise within three hours of bedtime.

## INCREASE SLEEP DRIVE

Recall that the neurotransmitter adenosine acts like air in a balloon. The more air in a balloon, the greater pressure it exerts. Likewise, the more adenosine in your sleep balloon, the greater your sleep pressure/sleep drive. These steps can increase your adenosine.

1. Nap only for sleepiness, not to make up for lost sleep, except in severe cases. Restrict naps to less than thirty minutes and take them before mid-afternoon. If you have a significant sleep deficit, go to bed a few minutes earlier than normal.

2. Limit caffeine. Caffeine stays in your system several hours, so drink that last cup of coffee before noon.

3. Increase daily physical activity. Activity will put adenosine into your sleep balloon and increase sleep drive.

4. Go to bed when sleepy. Don't get a "head start" on sleep when you don't feel sleepy.

5. If you struggle with insomnia, slowly reduce time in bed to match your actual sleep time more closely. Record your bedtime and when you wake up in the morning. Estimate how long you stayed awake during the night. Smartwatches can help you record these data. Divide sleep time by total time in bed to get a sleep efficiency score. A good sleep efficiency ranges from 85 to 95 percent. Poor sleepers score around 65 percent. If you try this step, don't reduce your time in bed to less than six hours. As your sleep efficiency rises to a consistent 85 percent plus, expand your time in bed until your sleep efficiency drops. At that point, you've found your sweet spot for time in bed.

## REINFORCE YOUR SLEEP CLOCK

Earlier I explained how your sleep clock tells your body to release the sleep hormone, melatonin. The steps below can help you align your natural sleep rhythms to maximize the effects from melatonin.

1. Try to match your daily routines to your chronotype (morning or evening types). Larks (early to bed, early to rise) should schedule demanding tasks in the early morning. Owls (late to bed and later sleepers) should schedule theirs later in the day.

2. Limit screen use beginning at least one hour prior to bedtime. Many computers and handhelds include settings that turn down

blue light. Turn those settings on for nighttime use. Also, consider using blue-light-blocking glasses at night.

3. Dim your house lights an hour prior to bedtime.

4. Get a few minutes of morning sunlight to kick start your sleep clock. In winter consider using a light box. If you spend all your time indoors, you won't get adequate light exposure. Sunrise provides 10,000 luxes of light, whereas a brightly lit room only provides 500 luxes of light.

5. Create a relaxing pre-bed routine. Relaxation produces a brain wave similar to stage 1 sleep, the transition stage between waking and sleeping.[38] A hot shower one to two hours prior to bed can help lower your core temperature. Hot water expands the blood vessels in your hands and feet, which releases heat and helps reduce your body's core temperature, necessary for good sleep. Also, don't work on mentally demanding tasks two hours prior to bedtime, and pray as you go to bed.

## DECREASE MENTAL AND EMOTIONAL AROUSAL

Arousal close to bedtime can inhibit good sleep. These suggestions can help limit evening arousal.

1. Reserve the bed only for sleep and sex. Don't work, watch TV, or read from a screen while in bed. Those activities become wakefulness cues rather than sleep cues. Train yourself to see the bed as a cue for sleep, not as a cue for another activity.

2. When you can't sleep at night because your mind is too active, don't force sleep or try a little harder to sleep. Apply the 30–30 rule, which means to get up after thirty minutes of tossing and tumbling (estimate it). Then, do a calm activity. Read from a paper

book, watch a boring TV show, or fold clothes. After thirty minutes, go back to bed. This may seem counterintuitive, but research tells a different story. The longer you lie in bed, toss and turn, and try to force yourself asleep, the longer you will lie awake.[39]

3. If you struggle with negative sleep thoughts, use a thought records chart to capture and replace negative sleep thoughts with positive sleep thoughts. Not only does actual sleep loss affect us, but our perceptions about sleep loss do as well. Negative sleep thoughts might include these: "I must get eight hours of sleep." "I dread bedtime." "I won't be able to function tomorrow because I'm not sleeping well." Restful sleep will come easier when you eliminate negative sleep thoughts.

4. Schedule a time during the day when you put on paper issues that may cause you worry and don't bring those worries to bed. Research shows that when we worry right before bedtime, we don't fall asleep as quickly, don't sleep as well, and wake up more often.[40]

5. Practice biblical mindfulness. My book *Holy Noticing* explains a biblical approach to mindfulness.

This chapter, Practice 9: Sleep Smart, covered many sleep ideas. Experiment with steps from the Sleep Box to see which ones might help you sleep better. Remember, healthy sleep cushions the negative effects from chronic stress.

In the final chapter, I pull all the practices together and challenge you to apply what you have learned.

## REVIEW

*Big idea:* Prioritize healthy sleep habits to cushion the effects from chronic stress.

*Bible insight:* The Bible references sleep more than one hundred times.

*Brain insight:* Good sleep habits maximize the positive benefits from your brain's sleep chemicals.

*Best practice:* The Four-Stage Sleep Box Strategy.

### APPLICATION

1. What connections can you make between what Scripture says about sleep and the science of good sleep?

2. What factors hinder your ability to sleep well? What quadrant from the Sleep Box relates most to those sleep struggles?

3. Review the ideas in each quadrant of the Sleep Box and pick one suggestion from each quadrant to try this week. How might they help you sleep better?

4. Which one do you think could improve your sleep the most? Why? How can you incorporate it into your daily routine, and how can you determine if it helped?

Complete your Stress Resilience Plan.

Downloadable tools available here: www.charlesstone.com/stress.

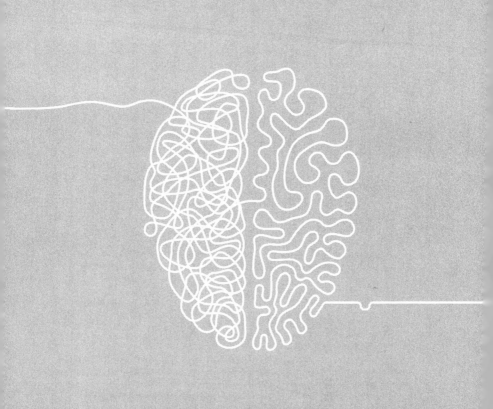

# Final Thoughts

*Our souls thrive not on accomplishments,
but on connection with God. In this connection,
we find true rest and stress finds no room.*

**DALLAS WILLARD**
*philosopher and writer (1925–2013)*

Throughout this book, we've covered significant ground as we have viewed stress resilience through a biblical, brain science, and best practices lens. You've developed your personal Stress Resilience Growth Plan. These nine practices, nine big ideas, and nine best practices provided the core for your plan.

## PRACTICE 1: CEASE AND BREATHE.

*Big Idea:* Leverage your breath to enhance your resilience.

*Best Practice:* The STOPP resilience building skill.

## PRACTICE 2: REVEAL HOW YOU FEEL.

*Big Idea:* Resolve unpleasant emotions before chronic stress develops.

*Best Practice:* Notice, Name, and Distance.

### PRACTICE 3: BROADEN AND BUILD.

*Big Idea:* Increase experiences that satisfy to offset the stress from experiences that deplete.

*Best Practice:* The Pleasure Piggy Bank.

### PRACTICE 4: AUDIT YOUR THOUGHTS.

*Big Idea:* Reinforce positive thoughts and redirect negative ones to fortify your resilience.

*Best Practice:* The START cognitive control process.

### PRACTICE 5: SOAK YOUR SOUL.

*Big Idea:* Nurture your soul to combat the stress that stems from spiritual dryness.

*Best Practice:* The four concepts reflected in CASI.

### PRACTICE 6: CULTIVATE CERTAINTY.

*Big Idea:* Boost your tolerance to uncertainty to increase your tolerance to stress.

*Best Practice:* Surrendering prayer.

### PRACTICE 7: GROW GRATITUDE.

*Big Idea:* Grow your gratitude to stifle your stress.

*Best Practice:* Three Good Things.

### PRACTICE 8: SAFEGUARD SAFETY.

*Big Idea:* Develop and protect safe relationships to enhance your well-being and resilience.

*Best Practice:* Build relationships with HEART.

### PRACTICE 9: SLEEP SMART.

*Big Idea:* Prioritize healthy sleep habits to cushion the effects from chronic stress.

*Best Practice:* The Four-Stage Sleep Box Strategy.

You may also receive several downloadable tools to help you grow your stress resilience. You can access them here: www.charlesstone.com/stress.

Brain science and best practices help us understand and grow our stress resilience. Ultimately, though, the Bible points to Jesus as the perfect source for wisdom and strength to grow resilience.

His grace suffices to meet our needs when stressed (2 Cor. 12:9).

He gives us the strength we need to bear with and triumph over every stressor (Phil. 4:19).

He is the anchor for our souls when stress weighs us down (Heb. 6:19).

He uses the stressful difficulties in life to make us more like Him (2 Cor. 12:10).

Jesus promises us joy even in the most stressful situations (John 15:11).

Keep Him at the forefront as you grow through stress. Let this final Scripture give you hope as you do: "Come to me, all of you who are weary and carry heavy burdens, and I will give you rest" (Matt. 11:28 NLT).

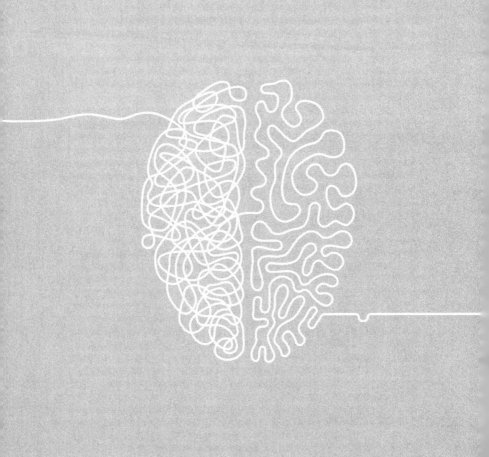

# Notes

**INTRODUCTION**

1. "More than a Quarter of U.S. Adults Say They're So Stressed They Can't Function," *American Psychological Association*, October 19, 2022, https://www.apa.org/news/**press**/releases/2022/10/multiple-stressors-no-function.
2. Diego Fernandez-Duque et al., "Superfluous Neuroscience Information Makes Explanations of Psychological Phenomena More Appealing," *Journal of Cognitive Neuroscience* 27, no. 5 (2015): 926–44, https://doi.org/10.1162/jocn_a_00750.

**CHAPTER 1: WHAT STRESS IS**

1. Telle Hailikari et. al, "The Relevance of Prior Knowledge in Learning and Instructional Design," *American Journal of Pharmaceutical Education* 72, no. 5 (2008): 113, https://www.ncbi.nlm.nih.gov/pmc/articles/PMC2630138/.
2. Richard Lazarus and Susan Folkman, "Transactional Theory and Research on Emotions and Coping," *European Journal of Personality* 1, no. 3 (1987): 141–69, https://doi.org/10.1002/per.2410010304.
3. Jane K. Ferguson et al., "Centering Prayer as a Healing Response to Everyday Stress: A Psychological and Spiritual Process," *Pastoral Psychology* 59, no. 3 (2010): 314, https://doi.org/10.1007/s11089-009-0225-7.
4. Richard S. Lazarus, *Stress and Emotion: A New Synthesis* (New York: Springer, 1999).
5. Kelly McGonigal, *The Upside of Stress: Why Stress Is Good for You, and How to Get Good at It* (New York: Avery, 2015), 84.
6. Adriana Feder et al., "The Biology of Human Resilience: Opportunities for Enhancing Resilience Across the Life Span," *Biological Psychiatry* 86, no. 6 (2019): 446, https://doi.org/10.1016/j.biopsych.2019.07.012.
7. W. Willaert et al., "Combining Stress Management With Pain Neuroscience Education and Exercise Therapy in People With Whiplash-Associated Disorders: A Clinical Perspective," *Physical Therapy* 101, no. 7 (2021): pzab105, https://doi.org/10.1093/ptj/pzab105.
8. Adriaan Louw et al., "The Effect of Neuroscience Education on Pain, Disability, Anxiety, and Stress in Chronic Musculoskeletal Pain," *Archives of Physical Medicine and Rehabilitation* 92, no. 12 (2011): 2041–56, https://doi.org/10.1016/j.apmr.2011.07.198.
9. Golnaz Tabibnia and Dan Radecki, "Resilience Training That Can Change the Brain," *Consulting Psychology Journal: Practice and Research* 70, no. 1 (2018): 59–88, https://doi.org/10.1037/cpb0000110.
10. Amit Sood, *SMART with Dr. Sood: The Four-Module Stress Management And Resilience Training Program* (Rochester, MN: Global Center for Resiliency and Wellbeing, 2019).
11. Sood, *SMART*.
12. Nelson and Simmons, "Health Psychology and Work Stress."
13. Debra L. Nelson and Bret L. Simmons, "Healthy Psychology and Work Stress: A More Positive Approach," in *Handbook of Occupational Health Psychology*, eds. J. C. Quick and L. E. Tetrick (American Psychological Association, 2003), 97–119, https://doi.org/10.1037/10474-005.
14. Barbara Oakley et al., *Uncommon Sense Teaching: Practical Insights in Brain Science to Help Students Learn* (New York: TarcherPerigee, 2021), 181–82.
15. Oakley et al., *Uncommon Sense Teaching*.

16. Robert W. Gauger, "Understanding the Internal, External, and Spiritual Factors of Stress and Depression in Clergy Serving the Southside of Jacksonville, Florida" (PhD diss., Regent University, 2011), ProQuest (3515319).

17. Jonathan T. Pennington, "A Biblical Theology of Human Flourishing," *Institute for Faith, Work & Economics*, March 4, 2015, https://tifwe.org/resource/a-biblical-theology-of-human-flourishing-2/.

18. Wayne E. Oates, "Stress Perception and Management in the Pastor's Life and Work," *Review & Expositor* 83, no. 4 (1986): 573–85, https://doi.org/10.1177/003463738608300406.

19. Oates, "Stress Perception," 575.

20. Oates, "Stress Perception," 576.

21. Oates, "Stress Perception," 578.

22. Oates, "Stress Perception," 580.

## CHAPTER 2: WHAT STRESS DOES

1. Kirk D. Strosahl and Patricia J. Robinson, *In This Moment: Five Steps to Transcending Stress Using Mindfulness and Neuroscience* (Oakland, CA: New Harbinger Publications, 2015), 9.

2. Bronwyn Fryer, "Are You Working Too Hard?" *Harvard Business Review*, November 2005, https://hbr.org/2005/11/are-you-working-too-hard.

3. Suzanne C. Segerstrom and Gregory E. Miller, "Psychological Stress and the Human Immune System: A Meta-Analytic Study of 30 Years of Inquiry," *Psychological Bulletin* 130, no. 4 (2004): 601–30, https://doi.org/10.1037/0033-2909.130.4.601.

4. Armita Golkar et al., "The Influence of Work-Related Chronic Stress on the Regulation of Emotion and on Functional Connectivity in the Brain," *PLOS ONE* 9, no. 9 (2014): e104550, https://doi.org/10.1371/journal.pone.0104550.

5. Kerry J. Ressler, "Amygdala Activity, Fear, and Anxiety: Modulation by Stress," *Biological Psychiatry* 67, no. 12 (2010): 1117–19, https://doi.org/10.1016/j.biopsych.2010.04.027.

6. Amy F. T. Arnsten et al., "The Effects of Stress Exposure on Prefrontal Cortex: Translating Basic Research into Successful Treatments for Post-Traumatic Stress Disorder," *Neurobiology of Stress* 1 (2015): 89–99, https://doi.org/10.1016/j.ynstr.2014.10.002.

7. Sandra Blakeslee, "A Small Part of the Brain, and Its Profound Effects," *New York Times*, February 6, 2007, https://www.nytimes.com/2007/02/06/health/psychology/06brain.html.

8. This is called interoception. Hideyuki Takahashi et al., "The Anterior Insula Tracks Behavioral Entropy during an Interpersonal Competitive Game," *PLOS ONE* 10, no. 6 (2015), https://doi.org/10.1371/journal.pone.0123329.

9. Ressler, "Amygdala Activity, Fear, and Anxiety."

10. Roy F. Baumeister et al., "Bad Is Stronger than Good," *Review of General Psychology* 5, no. 4 (2001): 323–70, https://doi.org/10.1037/1089-2680.5.4.323.

11. Steve Peters, *The Chimp Paradox: The Mind Management Program to Help You Achieve Success, Confidence, and Happiness* (New York: TarcherPerigee, 2013).

12. Stephen W. Porges, "The Polyvagal Theory: New Insights into Adaptive Reactions of the Autonomic Nervous System," *Cleveland Clinic Journal of Medicine* 76, no. 4 suppl 2 (2009): S86–90, https://doi.org/10.3949/ccjm.76.s2.17.

13. Amit Sood, *Stronger: The Science and Art of Stress Resilience* (Rochester, MN: Global Center for Resiliency and Wellbeing, 2018), 58.

14. Charles Stone, *Holy Noticing: The Bible, Your Brain, and the Mindful Space Between Moments* (Chicago: Moody, 2019), 82–86. Material adapted by permission.

15. Elyse R. Park et al., "The Development of a Patient-Centered Program Based on the Relaxation Response: The Relaxation Response Resiliency Program (3RP)," *Psychosomatics* 54, no. 2 (2013): 165–74, https://doi.org/10.1016/j.psym.2012.09.001.

16. B. S. McEwen, "Allostasis and Allostatic Load: Implications for Neuropsychopharmacology," *Neuropsychopharmacology: Official Publication of the American College of Neuropsychopharmacology* 22, no. 2 (2000): 108–24, https://doi.org/10.1016/S0893-133X(99)00129-3.

17. McEwen, "Allostasis and Allostatic Load," 368.

18. Randy Garner, "Interpersonal Criticism and the Clergy," *Journal of Pastoral Care & Counseling* 67, no. 1 (2013): 1–14, https://doi.org/10.1177/154230501306700102.

19. Agorastos Agorastos et al., "Developmental Trajectories of Early Life Stress and Trauma: A Narrative Review on Neurobiological Aspects Beyond Stress System Dysregulation," *Frontiers in Psychiatry* 10 (2019): 118, https://doi.org/10.3389/fpsyt.2019.00118.

20. Talya Greene et al., "Psychological Trauma and Moral Injury in Religious Leaders During COVID-19," *Psychological Trauma* 12, no. S1 (2020): S143–45, https://doi.org/10.1037/tra0000641.

21. Jason Castro, "A Wandering Mind Is an Unhappy One," *Scientific American*, November 24, 2010, http://www.scientificamerican.com/article.cfm?id=a-wandering-mind-is-an-un.

22. Janet Durkee-Lloyd, "The Relationship Between Work-Related Psychological Health and Psychological Type Among Canadian Baptist Clergy: A Research Report," *Journal of Empirical Theology* 29, no. 2 (2016): 201–11, https://doi.org/10.1163/15709256–12341343.

23. Jeromy Anglim et al., "Predicting Psychological and Subjective Well-Being from Personality," *Psychological Bulletin* 146, no. 4 (2015): 309, https://doi.org/10.1037/bul0000226.

24. Tena Vukasović and Denis Bratko, "Heritability of Personality: A Meta-Analysis of Behavior Genetic Studies," *Psychological Bulletin* 141, no. 4 (2015): 769–85, https://doi.org/10.1037/bul0000017.

25. Sood, *Stronger*, 37.

26. Steven M. Southwick and Dennis S. Charney, *Resilience: The Science of Mastering Life's Greatest Challenges*, 2nd ed. (Cambridge: Cambridge University Press, 2018), 47.

27. Joseph A. Stewart-Sicking et al., "Workplace Characteristics, Career/Vocation Satisfaction, and Existential Well-Being in Episcopal Clergy," *Mental Health, Religion & Culture* 14, no. 7 (2010): 715–30, https://doi.org/10.1080/13674676.2010.516428.

28. Mithu Storoni, *Stress-Proof: The Ultimate Guide to Living a Stress-Free Life* (London: Yellow Kite, 2019), 152.

29. Storoni, *Stress-Proof*, 153.

30. Habib Yaribeygi et al., "The Impact of Stress on Body Function: A Review," *EXCLI Journal* 16 (2017): 1057–72, https://doi.org/10.17179/excli2017–480.

31. J. J. Radley et al., "Chronic Behavioral Stress Induces Apical Dendritic Reorganization in Pyramidal Neurons of the Medial Prefrontal Cortex," *Neuroscience* 125, no. 1 (2004): 1–6, https://doi.org/10.1016/j.neuroscience.2004.01.006.

32. Ajai Vyas et al., "Chronic Stress Induces Contrasting Patterns of Dendritic Remodeling in Hippocampal and Amygdaloid Neurons," *Journal of Neuroscience* 22, no. 15 (2002): 6810–18, https://doi.org/10.1523/JNEUROSCI.22–15–06810.2002.

33. V. Pinto et al., "Differential Impact of Chronic Stress Along the Hippocampal Dorsal-Ventral Axis," *Brain Structure & Function* 220, no. 2 (2015): 1205–12, https://doi.org/10.1007/s00429–014–0713–0.

34. Radley et al., "Chronic Behavioral Stress."

35. Storoni, *Stress-Proof*, xix.

36. Anthony J. Ocon, "Caught in the Thickness of Brain Fog: Exploring the Cognitive Symptoms of Chronic Fatigue Syndrome," *Frontiers in Physiology* 4 (2013): 63, https://doi.org/10.3389/fphys.2013.00063.

37. Georgina L. Moreno et al., "Increased Perceived Stress Is Related to Decreased Prefrontal Cortex Volumes Among Older Adults," *Journal of Clinical and Experimental Neuropsychology* 39, no. 4 (2016): 313–25, https://doi.org/10.1080/13803395.2016.1225006.

38. Raffael Kalisch et al., "A Conceptual Framework for the Neurobiological Study of Resilience," *Behavioral and Brain Sciences* 38 (2015): e92, doi:10.1017/S0140525X1400082X.

39. P. D. Harms et al., "Leadership and Stress: A Meta-Analytic Review," *The Leadership Quarterly* 28, no. 1 (2017): 178, https://doi.org/10.1016/j.leaqua.2016.10.006.

40. Christina Maslach, *Burnout: The Cost of Caring* (Englewood Cliffs, NJ: Malor Books, 2011).

41. Maslach, *Burnout*, 397.

42. Maslach, *Burnout*, 397.

43. Diane Chandler, "Pastoral Burnout and the Impact of Personal Spiritual Renewal, Rest-Taking, and Support System Practices," *Pastoral Psychology* 58, no. 3 (2009): 273–87, https://doi.org/10.1007/s11089–008–0184–4.

44. Depersonalization was Maslach's "cynicism"; reduced accomplishment, Maslach's "inefficacy."

45. Anne-Laure Le Cunff, "Burnout or Boreout?," *Ness Labs* (blog), September 26, 2023, https://nesslabs.com/burnout-vs-boreout.

46. Bryan Lufkin, "The Damaging Effects of 'Boreout' at Work," July 4, 2021, https://www.bbc.com/worklife/article/20210701-the-damaging-effects-of-boreout-at-work; Lotta Harju et al., "Job Boredom and Its Correlates in 87 Finnish Organizations," *Journal of Occupational and Environmental Medicine* 56, no. 9 (2014): 911–18, https://doi.org/10.1097/

JOM.0000000000000248; A. Abubakar et al., "Burnout or Boreout: A Meta-Analytic Review and Synthesis of Burnout and Boreout Literature in Hospitality and Tourism," *Journal of Hospitality Marketing & Management* 31, no. 4 (2021): 458–503, https://doi.org/10.1080/193 68623.2022.1996304.

## CHAPTER 3: WHAT RESILIENCE IS AND WHAT IT DOES

1. Kathryn Connor and Jonathan Davidson, "Development of a New Resilience Scale: The Connor-Davidson Resilience Scale (CD-RISC)," *Depression and Anxiety* 18 (2003): 77, https://doi.org/10.1002/da.10113.

2. Daniel Goleman et al., *Resilience* (Brighton, MA: Harvard Business Review Press, 2017).

3. Cindy A. Kermott et al., "Is Higher Resilience Predictive of Lower Stress and Better Mental Health among Corporate Executives?," *PLOS ONE* 14, no. 6 (2019): e0218092, https://doi.org/10.1371/journal.pone.0218092.

4. Rick Hanson and Forrest Hanson, *Resilient: How to Grow an Unshakable Core of Calm, Strength, and Happiness* (New York: Harmony, 2018), 155.

5. Amit Sood, *Stronger: The Science and Art of Stress Resilience* (Rochester, MN: Global Center for Resiliency and Wellbeing, 2018).

6. Sood, *Stronger*, 20.

7. "Building Your Resilience," *American Psychological Association*, updated February 1, 2020, https://www.apa.org/topics/resilience/building-your-resilience.

8. Steven M. Southwick and Dennis S. Charney, *Resilience: The Science of Mastering Life's Greatest Challenges*, 2nd ed. (Cambridge: Cambridge University Press, 2018), 8.

9. Jonathan T. Pennington, "A Biblical Theology of Human Flourishing," *Institute for Faith, Work & Economics*, March 4, 2015, https://tifwe.org/resource/a-biblical-theology-of-human-flourishing-2/, 5.

10. Pennington, "A Biblical Theology," 16.

11. Southwick, *Resilience*, 25.

12. Sonja Lyubomirsky et al., "Pursuing Happiness: The Architecture of Sustainable Change," *Review of General Psychology* 9, no. 2 (2005): 111–31, https://doi.org/10.1037/1089-2680.9.2.111.

13. Golnaz Tabibnia and Dan Radecki, "Resilience Training That Can Change the Brain," *Consulting Psychology Journal: Practice and Research* 70, no. 1 (2018): 78, https://doi.org/10.1037/cpb0000110; Adriana Feder et al., "Psychobiology and Molecular Genetics of Resilience," *Nature Reviews Neuroscience* 10, no. 6 (2009): 446–57, https://doi.org/10.1038/nrn2649; Raffael Kalisch et al., "A Conceptual Framework for the Neurobiological Study of Resilience," *Behavioral and Brain Sciences* 38 (2015): 1–21, doi:10.1017/S0140525X1400082X.

14. Barbara L. Fredrickson, "The Broaden-and-Build Theory of Positive Emotions," Philosophical *Transactions of the Royal Society B: Biological Sciences* 359, no. 1449 (2004): 1371, https://doi.org/10.1098/rstb.2004.1512.

15. Tabibnia and Radecki, "Resilience Training," 59, 78.

16. Tabibnia and Radecki, "Resilience Training," 74.

17. Jurie Rossouw et al., "Building Resilience Through a Virtual Coach Called Driven: Longitudinal Pilot Study and the Neuroscience of Small, Frequent Learning Tasks," *International Journal of Neuropsychotherapy* 7, no. 2 (2019): 23.

18. Debra L. Nelson and Bret L. Simmons, "Healthy Psychology and Work Stress: A More Positive Approach," in *Handbook of Occupational Health Psychology*, eds. J. C. Quick and L. E. Tetrick, American Psychological Association (2003): 97–119, https://doi.org/10.1037/10474-005.

19. Goleman et al., *Resilience*, 13.

20. Viktor E. Frankl, *Man's Search for Meaning* (Boston: Beacon Press, 2006).

21. Elyse R. Park et al., "The Development of a Patient-Centered Program Based on the Relaxation Response: The Relaxation Response Resiliency Program (3RP)," *Psychosomatics* 54, no. 2 (2013): 171, https://doi.org/10.1016/j.psym.2012.09.001.

22. Goleman et al., *Resilience*, 64.

23. Steven C. Cramer et al., "Harnessing Neuroplasticity for Clinical Applications," *Brain* 134,

no. 6 (2011): 1591–1609, https://doi.org/10.1093/brain/awr039.

24. Marcus Grueschow et al., "Real-World Stress Resilience Is Associated with the Responsivity of the Locus Coeruleus," *Nature Communications* 12, no. 1 (2021): 2275, https://doi.org/10.1038/s41467–021–22509–1.

25. Dávid Farkas and Gábor Orosz, "Ego-Resiliency Reloaded: A Three-Component Model of General Resiliency," *PLOS ONE* 10, no. 3 (2015): e0120883, https://doi.org/10.1371/journal.pone.0120883.

26. Sood, *Stronger*, 62–69.

27. Sood, *Stronge*r, 62–69.

28. Jean-Philippe Gouin et al., "Resilience Resources Moderate the Association of Adverse Childhood Experiences with Adulthood Inflammation," *Annals of Behavioral Medicine* 51, no. 5 (2017): 782–86, https://doi.org/10.1007/s12160–017–9891–3.

29. Fatih Ozbay et al., "Social Support and Resilience to Stress," *Psychiatry (Edgmont)* 4, no. 5 (2007): 35–40.

## CHAPTER 4: PRACTICE 1: CEASE AND BREATHE

1. Joanna J. Arch and Michelle G. Craske, "Mechanisms of Mindfulness: Emotion Regulation Following a Focused Breathing Induction," *Behaviour Research and Therapy* 44, no. 12 (2006), 1849–58, https://doi.org/10.1016/j.brat.2005.12.007.

2. Vblaban, "How Much Air Do We Breathe in a Lifetime?," *The Tipsters* (blog), January 5, 2013, https://thetipsters.wordpress.com/2013/01/05/how-much-air-do-we-breathe-in-a-lifetime/.

3. Alex Korb, *The Upward Spiral: Using Neuroscience to Reverse the Course of Depression, One Small Change at a Time* (Oakland, CA: New Harbinger Publications, 2015).

4. Xiao Ma et al., "The Effect of Diaphragmatic Breathing on Attention, Negative Affect and Stress in Healthy Adults," *Frontiers in Psychology* 8 (2017): https://doi.org/10.3389/fpsyg.2017.00874.

5. Korb, *The Upward Spiral*, 148.

6. Yanhui Liao et al., Brief Mindfulness-Based Intervention of 'STOP (Stop, Take a Breath, Observe, Proceed) Touching Your Face': A Study Protocol of a Randomised Controlled Trial, *BMJ Open* 10, no. 11 (2020): e041364, doi: 10.1136/bmjopen-2020-041364.

7. Bill Gaultiere, "Statio: Pausing to Be Prayerful," *Soul Shepherding*, December 13, 2021, https://www.soulshepherding.org/statio-pausing-to-be-prayerful/.

8. "The Ruthless Elimination of Hurry," *Unhurried Living*, accessed November 20, 2023, https://www.unhurriedliving.com/blog/ruthless-elimination-of-hurry.

9. Ashley Lyon, "What Does Selah Mean?," *Word by Word*, January 24, 2023, https://www.logos.com/grow/bsm-what-does-selah-mean/.

10. WebMD Editorial Contributors, "What to Know About 4-7-8 Breathing," *WebMD*, June 27, 2023, https://www.webmd.com/balance/what-to-know-4-7-8-breathing.

11. Noma Nazish, "How To De-Stress In 5 Minutes Or Less, According To A Navy SEAL," *Forbes*, updated Dec 10, 2021, https://www.forbes.com/sites/nomanazish/2019/05/30/how-to-de-stress-in-5-minutes-or-less-according-to-a-navy-seal/.

12. Dilwar Hussain, "Meta-Cognition in Mindfulness: A Conceptual Analysis," *Psychological Thought* 8, no. 2 (2015): 132–41, https://doi.org/10.23668/psycharchives.1972.

13. Jennifer A. Livingston, "Metacognition: An Overview" (ERIC Clearinghouse, 2003).

14. G. E. H. Palmer et al., trans., *Philokalia: The Eastern Christian Spiritual Texts* (Woodstock, VT: SkyLight Paths, 2006).

15. Kate Cavanagh et al., "A Randomised Controlled Trial of a Brief Online Mindfulness-Based Intervention," *Behaviour Research and Therapy* 51, no. 9 (2013): 573–78, https://doi.org/10.1016/j.brat.2013.06.003.

## CHAPTER 5: PRACTICE 2: REVEAL HOW YOU FEEL

1. Jeremy Dean, "Why Thought Suppression Is Counter-Productive," *Psyblog*, May 22, 2009, http://www.spring.org.uk/2009/05/why-thought-suppression-is-counter-productive.php.

2. Rhyne Putman, "9 Ways Emotions Play a Role in Theological Diversity," *Crossway*, May 24, 2020, https://www.crossway.org/articles/9-ways-emotions-play-a-role-in-theological-diversity/.

3. Putman, "9 Ways."

4. Putman, "9 Ways."

5. Putman, "9 Ways."

6. Timothy Keller, "Four Models of Counseling in Pastoral Ministry," Gospel in Life, May 12, 2010, https://gospelinlife.com/manual-paper/four-models-of-counseling-in-pastoral-ministry/.

7. James J. Gross, "Emotion Regulation: Current Status and Future Prospects," *Psychological Inquiry* 26, no. 1 (2015): 1–26, https://doi.org/10.1080/1047840X.2014.940781.

8. Maurice Topper et al., "Are Rumination and Worry Two Sides of the Same Coin? A Structural Equation Modelling Approach," *Journal of Experimental Psychopathology* 5, no. 3 (2014): 363–81, https://doi.org/10.5127/jep.038813.

9. Jeromy Anglim et al., "Predicting Psychological and Subjective Well-Being from Personality: A Meta-Analysis," *Psychological Bulletin 146*, no. 4 (2020): 279–323, https://doi.org/10.1037/bul0000226.

10. Richard J. Davidson and Sharon Begley, *The Emotional Life of Your Brain* (New York: Hudson Street Press, 2012).

11. Rae Jean Proeschold-Bell, *Faithful and Fractured* (Grand Rapids, MI: Baker Academic, 2018), 109.

12. Bruce Headey, "Life Goals Matter to Happiness: A Revision of Set-Point Theory," *Social Indicators Research* 86, no. 2 (2008): 213–31, https://doi.org/10.1007/s11205–007–9138-y.

13. Adriana Feder et al., "Psychobiology and Molecular Genetics of Resilience," *Nature Reviews Neuroscience* 10, no. 6 (2009): 446–57, https://doi.org/10.1038/nrn2649.

14. Robin John Snelgar et al., "Preventing Compassion Fatigue Amongst Pastors: The Influence of Spiritual Intelligence and Intrinsic Motivation," *Journal of Psychology & Theology* 45, no. 4 (2017): 258, https://doi.org/10.1177/009164711704500401.

15. Armita Golkar et al., "The Influence of Work-Related Chronic Stress on the Regulation of Emotion and on Functional Connectivity in the Brain," *PLOS ONE* 9, no. 9 (2014): e104550, https://doi.org/10.1371/journal.pone.0104550.

16. Leonard Mlodinow, *Emotional: How Feelings Shape Our Thinking* (New York: Pantheon, 2022), 8.

17. Anglim et al., "Predicting Psychological and Subjective Well-Being."

18. Samantha Dockray and Andrew Steptoe, "Positive Affect and Psychobiological Processes," *Neuroscience and Biobehavioral Reviews* 35, no. 1 (2010): 69–75, https://doi.org/10.1016/j.neubiorev.2010.01.006.

19. Raffael Kalisch et al., "A Conceptual Framework for the Neurobiological Study of Resilience," *Behavioral and Brain Sciences* 38 (2015): 1–21, doi:10.1017/S0140525X1400082X.

20. Barbara L. Fredrickson, "The Broaden-and-Build Theory of Positive Emotions," *Philosophical Transactions of the Royal Society* B: *Biological Sciences* 359, no. 1449 (2004): 1371, https://doi.org/10.1098/rstb.2004.1512.

21. Thomas V. Frederick et al., "Burnout in Christian Perspective," *Pastoral Psychology* 67, no. 3 (2018): 267, https://doi.org/10.1007/s11089–017–0799–4.

22. Mlodinow, *Emotional*, 110.

23. Mlodinow, *Emotional*, 62.

24. Mlodinow, *Emotional*, 211.

25. Kirk D. Strosahl and Patricia J. Robinson, *In This Moment: Five Steps to Transcending Stress Using Mindfulness and Neuroscience* (Oakland, CA: New Harbinger Publications, 2015), 81.

26. Carolyn M. Schmitt and Sarah Schoen, "Interoception: A Multi-Sensory Foundation of Participation in Daily Life," *Frontiers in Neuroscience* 16 (2022): 875200, https://doi.org/10.3389/fnins.2022.875200.

27. Annie Murphy Paul, *The Extended Mind: The Power of Thinking Outside the Brain* (Boston: Mariner Books, 2021), 32.

28. Paul, *The Extended Mind*, 22–23.
29. Salvatore J. Torrisi et al., "Advancing Understanding of Affect Labeling with Dynamic Causal Modeling," *NeuroImage* 82 (2013): 481–88, https://doi.org/10.1016/j.neuroimage .2013.06.025.
30. Paul, *The Extended Mind*, 28.
31. Philippe R. Goldin et al., "The Neural Bases of Emotion Regulation: Reappraisal and Suppression of Negative Emotion," *Biological Psychiatry* 63, no. 6 (2008): 577–86, https://doi .org/10.1016/j.biopsych.2007.05.031.
32. Golnaz Tabibnia and Dan Radecki, "Resilience Training That Can Change the Brain," *Consulting Psychology Journal: Practice and Research* 70, no. 1 (2018): 69, https://doi.org/ 10.1037/cpb0000110.
33. Andrea N. Niles et al., "Affect Labeling Enhances Exposure Effectiveness for Public Speaking Anxiety," *Behaviour Research and Therapy* 68 (2015): 27–36, https://doi.org/10.1016/j.brat .2015.03.004.
34. Todd B. Kashdan et al., "Unpacking Emotion Differentiation: Transforming Unpleasant Experience by Perceiving Distinctions in Negativity," *Current Directions in Psychological Science* 24, no. 1 (2015): 10–16, https://doi.org/10.1177/0963721414550708.
35. Alicia A. Grandey et al., "Emotional Labor Threatens Decent Work: A Proposal to Eradicate Emotional Display Rules," *Journal of Organizational Behavior* 36, no. 6 (2015): 770–85, https://doi.org/10.1002/job.2020.
36. Steven C Hayes, *Get Out of Your Mind and Into Your Life: The New Acceptance and Commitment Therapy* (Oakland, CA: New Harbinger Publications, 2005).
37. Ethan Kross, Chatter: *The Voice in Our Head, Why It Matters, and How to Harness It* (New York: Crown, 2021), 73.
38. Jason S. Moser et al., "Third-Person Self-Talk Facilitates Emotion Regulation Without Engaging Cognitive Control: Converging Evidence from ERP and fMRI," *Scientific Reports* 7, no. 1 (2017): 4519, https://doi.org/10.1038/s41598–017–04047–3.
39. Kross, *Chatter*, 48.
40. Kross, *Chatter*, 61.
41. James W. Pennebaker, "Expressive Writing in Psychological Science," *Perspectives on Psychological Science* 13, no. 2 (2018): 226–29, https://doi.org/10.1177/1745691617707315.
42. Clement Yong Hao Lau and William Tov, "Effects of Positive Reappraisal and Self-Distancing on the Meaningfulness of Everyday Negative Events," *Frontiers in Psychology* 14 (2023): 1093412, https://doi.org/10.3389/fpsyg.2023.1093412.

## CHAPTER 6: PRACTICE 3: BROADEN AND BUILD

1. Barbara L. Fredrickson, "Leading with Positive Emotions," Center for Positive Organizations, n.d., https://positiveorgs.bus.umich.edu/wp-content/uploads/CPOSweb-TryingTimes-Fredrickson-PositiveEmotions.pdf.
2. William Martin Miller, "The Selected and Perceived Factors of Depression and Burnout in Charles Haddon Spurgeon's Ministry with a Contemporary Application" (PhD diss., Southeastern Baptist Theological Seminary, 2020), 247, https://search.proquest.com/ docview/2395792360/abstract/15165DD981A4734PQ/11.
3. Barbara L. Fredrickson, "The Broaden-and-Build Theory of Positive Emotions.," *Philosophical Transactions of the Royal Society B: Biological Sciences* 359, no. 1449 (2004): 1367–78, https:// doi.org/10.1098/rstb.2004.1512.
4. Jennifer Danilowski, "How Can Fredrickson's Broaden-and-Build Theory Enhance Personal Resources?," Digital Commons, Florida International University, 2015, https:// digitalcommons.fiu.edu/cgi/viewcontent.cgi?referer=&httpsredir=1&article=1429&context=sferc.
5. Mithu Storoni, *Stress-Proof: The Ultimate Guide to Living a Stress-Free Life* (London: Yellow Kite, 2019), 26.
6. Leonard Mlodinow, *Emotional: How Feelings Shape Our Thinking* (New York: Pantheon, 2022), 211.

7. Golnaz Tabibnia and Dan Radecki, "Resilience Training That Can Change the Brain," *Consulting Psychology Journal: Practice and Research* 70, no. 1 (2018): 64, https://doi.org/10.1037/cpb0000110.

8. Evian Gordon et al., "An 'Integrative Neuroscience' Platform: Application to Profiles of Negativity and Positivity Bias," *Journal of Integrative Neuroscience* 7, no. 3 (2008): 345–66, https://doi.org/10.1142/S0219635208001927.

9. F. Gregory Ashby et al., "A Neuropsychological Theory of Positive Affect and Its Influence on Cognition," *Psychological Review* 106, no. 3 (1999): 529–50, https://doi.org/10.1037/0033–295X.106.3.529.

10. Barbara L. Fredrickson and Thomas Joiner, "Reflections on Positive Emotions and Upward Spirals," *Perspectives on Psychological Science* 13, no. 2 (2018): 196, https://doi.org/10.1177/1745691617692106.

11. Fredrickson, "Broaden-and-Build Theory," 1373.

12. Barbara L. Fredrickson, "Updated Thinking on Positivity Ratios," *American Psychologist* 68, no. 9 (2013): 814–22, https://doi.org/10.1037/a0033584.

13. Fredrickson, "Broaden-and-Build Theory," 220.

14. Barbara L. Fredrickson, "The Role of Positive Emotions in Positive Psychology: The Broaden-and-Build Theory of Positive Emotions," *American Psychologist* 56, no. 3 (2001): 221, https://doi.org/10.1037/0003–066X.56.3.218.

15. Fredrickson, "Role of Positive Emotions," 220.

16. Barbara L. Fredrickson, "Cultivating Positive Emotions to Optimize Health and Well-Being," *Prevention & Treatment* 3, no. 1 (2000): Article 1, https://psycnet.apa.org/doi/10.1037/1522–3736.3.1.31a.

17. Fredrickson, "Broaden-and-Build Theory," 223.

18. Barbara L. Fredrickson et al., "The Undoing Effect of Positive Emotions," *Motivation and Emotion* 24, no. 4 (2000): 237–58, https://doi.org/10.1023/A:1010796329158.

19. Storoni, *Stress-Proof*, 151.

20. N. Geschwind et al., "Meeting Risk with Resilience: High Daily Life Reward Experience Preserves Mental Health," *Acta Psychiatrica Scandinavica* 122, no. 2 (2010): 129–38, https://doi.org/10.1111/j.1600–0447.2009.01525.x.

21. Storoni, *Stress-Proof*, 132.

22. Storoni, *Stress-Proof*, 152.

23. George S. Alexopoulos and Patricia Arean, "A Model for Streamlining Psychotherapy in the RDoC Era: The Example of 'Engage,'" *Molecular Psychiatry* 19, no. 1 (2014): 14–19, https://doi.org/10.1038/mp.2013.150.

**CHAPTER 7: PRACTICE 4: AUDIT YOUR THOUGHTS**

1. Julie Tseng and Jordan Poppenk, "Brain Meta-State Transitions Demarcate Thoughts Across Task Contexts Exposing the Mental Noise of Trait Neuroticism," *Nature Communications* 11, no. 1 (2020): 3480, https://doi.org/10.1038/s41467-020-17255-9.

2. Raj Raghunathan, "How Negative Is Your 'Mental Chatter'?," *Psychology Today*, October 10, 2013, https://www.psychologytoday.com/us/blog/sapient-nature/201310/how-negative-is-your-mental-chatter.

3. Jason Castro, "A Wandering Mind Is an Unhappy One," *Scientific American*, November 24, 2010, http://www.scientificamerican.com/article.cfm?id=a-wandering-mind-is-an-un.

4. Castro, "A Wandering Mind."

5. Steven C. Cramer et al., "Harnessing Neuroplasticity for Clinical Applications," *Brain* 134, no. 6 (2011): 1591–1609, https://doi.org/10.1093/brain/awr039.

6. Leonard Mlodinow, *Emotional: How Feelings Shape Our Thinking* (New York: Pantheon, 2022), 73.

7. Rick Hanson and Forrest Hanson, *Resilient: How to Grow an Unshakable Core of Calm, Strength, and Happiness* (New York: Harmony, 2018), 42.

8. Ana María Magariños et al., "Chronic Psychosocial Stress Causes Apical Dendritic Atrophy

of Hippocampal CA3 Pyramidal Neurons in Subordinate Tree Shrews," *The Journal of Neuroscience: The Official Journal of the Society for Neuroscience* 16, no. 10 (1996): 3534–40, https://doi.org/10.1523/JNEUROSCI.16-10-03534.1996.

9. Yuncai Chen et al., "Correlated Memory Defects and Hippocampal Dendritic Spine Loss After Acute Stress Involve Corticotropin-Releasing Hormone Signaling," *Proceedings of the National Academy of Sciences* 107, no. 29 (2010): 13123–28, https://doi.org/10.1073/pnas.1003825107.

10. I. D. Martijena and V. A. Molina, "The Influence of Stress on Fear Memory Processes," *Brazilian Journal of Medical and Biological Research* 45, no. 4 (2012): 308, https://doi.org/10.1590/S0100-879X2012007500045.

11. Shazia Veqar Siddiqui et al., "Neuropsychology of Prefrontal Cortex," *Indian Journal of Psychiatry* 50, no. 3 (2008): 202–8, https://doi.org/10.4103/0019-5545.43634.

12. Henry L. Thompson, *The Stress Effect: Why Smart Leaders Make Dumb Decisions—And What to Do About It* (San Francisco: Jossey-Bass, 2010), 153.

13. Amy F. T. Arnsten, "Stress Weakens Prefrontal Networks: Molecular Insults to Higher Cognition," *Nature Neuroscience* 18, no. 10 (2015): 1376, https://doi.org/10.1038/nn.4087.

14. Amishi P. Jha, *Peak Mind: Find Your Focus, Own Your Attention, Invest 12 Minutes a Day* (New York: HarperOne, 2021), 3.

15. Amit Sood, *Stronger: The Science and Art of Stress Resilience* (Rochester, MN: Global Center for Resiliency and Wellbeing, 2018), 29.

16. Anthony J. Porcelli and Mauricio R. Delgado, "Stress and Decision Making: Effects on Valuation, Learning, and Risk-Taking," *Current Opinion in Behavioral Sciences* 14 (2017): 33–39, https://doi.org/10.1016/j.cobeha.2016.11.015.

17. Dilwar Hussain, "Meta-Cognition in Mindfulness: A Conceptual Analysis," *Psychological Thought* 8, no. 2 (2015): 132–41, https://doi.org/10.23668/psycharchives.1972.

18. Jennifer A. Livingston, "Metacognition: An Overview" (ERIC Clearinghouse, 2003).

19. Mlodinow, *Emotional*, 37.

20. Timothy D. Wilson et al., "Just Think: The Challenges of the Disengaged Mind," *Science* 345, no. 6192 (2014): 75–77, https://doi.org/10.1126/science.1250830.

21. Marcus E. Raichle et al., "A Default Mode of Brain Function," *Proceedings of the National Academy of Sciences* 98, no. 2 (2001): 676–82, https://doi.org/10.1073/pnas.98.2.676.

22. Castro, "A Wandering Mind."

23. Rodney J. Korba, "The Rate of Inner Speech," *Perceptual and Motor Skills* 71, no. 3 (1990): 1043–52, https://doi.org/10.2466/PMS.71.7.1043-1052.

24. Matthew A. Killingsworth and Daniel T. Gilbert, "A Wandering Mind Is an Unhappy Mind," *Science* 330, no. 6006 (2010): 932, https://doi.org/10.1126/science.1192439.

25. Jos F. Brosschot, "Markers of Chronic Stress: Prolonged Physiological Activation and (Un) Conscious Perseverative Cognition," *Neuroscience and Biobehavioral Reviews* 35, no. 1 (2010): 46, https://doi.org/10.1016/j.neubiorev.2010.01.004.

26. Ethan Kross, *Chatter: The Voice in Our Head, Why It Matters, and How to Harness It* (New York: Crown, 2021), 41.

27. Kross, *Chatter*, 28.

28. Kross, *Chatter*, xvii.

29. Philip Parker and Andrew Martin, "Clergy Motivation and Occupational Well-Being: Exploring a Quadripolar Model and Its Role in Predicting Burnout and Engagement," *Journal of Religion & Health* 50, no. 3 (2011): 671, https://doi.org/10.1007/s10943-009-9303-5.

30. Cameron Lee and Judith Iverson-Gilbert, "Demand, Support, and Perception in Family-Related Stress Among Protestant Clergy," *Family Relations* 52, no. 3 (2003): 249, https://doi.org/10.1111/j.1741-3729.2003.00249.x.

31. Hanson and Hanson, *Resilient*, 136.

32. Joshua J. Knabb and Veola E. Vazquez, "A Randomized Controlled Trial of a 2-Week Internet-Based Contemplative Prayer Program for Christians with Daily Stress," *Spirituality in Clinical Practice* 5, no. 1 (2018): 37–53, https://doi.org/10.1037/scp0000154.

33. Adriana Feder et al., "The Biology of Human Resilience: Opportunities for Enhancing Resilience Across the Life Span," *Biological Psychiatry* 86, no. 6 (2019): 446, https://doi.org/10.1016/j.biopsych.2019.07.012.

34. Raffael Kalisch et al., "A Conceptual Framework for the Neurobiological Study of Resilience," *Behavioral and Brain Sciences* 38 (2015): 11, https://doi.org/10.1017/S0140525X1400082X.

35. Hanson and Hanson, *Resilient*, 139.

36. Thomas L. Webb et al., "Dealing with Feeling: A Meta-Analysis of the Effectiveness of Strategies Derived from the Process Model of Emotion Regulation," *Psychological Bulletin* 138, no. 4 (2012): 775–808, https://doi.org/10.1037/a0027600.

37. Martin Laird, *Into the Silent Land: A Guide to the Christian Practice of Contemplation* (Oxford University Press, 2006), loc. 287–93, Kindle; quoted in Charles Stone, "Arresting Anxiety when Spiritual Practices Fail, part 2," March 22, 2020, Crossmap, https://blogs.crossmap.com/stories/arresting-anxiety-when-spiritual-practices-fail-part-2---charles-stone-Tg5oLxWYlKzCXx0u0T51H.

38. Laird, *Into the Silent Land*, quoted in Stone, "Arresting Anxiety."

39. Eckhard Frick et al., "Do Self-Efficacy Expectation and Spirituality Provide a Buffer Against Stress-Associated Impairment of Health? A Comprehensive Analysis of the German Pastoral Ministry Study," *Journal of Religion and Health* 55, no. 2 (2016): 448–68, https://doi.org/10.1007/s10943-015-0040-7, 461.

40. Golnaz Tabibnia and Dan Radecki, "Resilience Training That Can Change the Brain," *Consulting Psychology Journal: Practice and Research* 70, no. 1 (2018): 64, https://doi.org/10.1037/cpb0000110.

41. Kross, *Chatter*, 78.

42. Sonya Parker, "Whatever You Focus Your Attention on Will Become Important to You Even If It's Unimportant," Search Quotes, accessed November 24, 2023, https://www.searchquotes.com/quotation/Whatever_you_focus_your_attention_on_will_become_important_to_you_even_if_it%27s_unimportant./737506/.

43. Jha, *Peak Mind*, 225.

44. Jha, *Peak Mind*, 12.

45. Chelsea Gill et al., "Applying Attention Restoration Theory to Understand and Address Clergy's Need to Restore Cognitive Capacity," *Journal of Religion & Health* 57, no. 5 (2018): 1779–92, https://doi.org/10.1007/s10943-018-0571-9.

46. Gill et al., "Applying Attention Restoration Theory."

47. Jha, *Peak Mind*, 37.

## CHAPTER 8: PRACTICE 5: SOAK YOUR SOUL

1. Jacek Prusak et al., "Spiritual Dryness Among People with Different Levels of Religious Commitment. Polish Adaptation of the Spiritual Dryness Scale: Psychometric Properties and Measurement Invariance," *Journal of Beliefs & Values* (2023): 1–18, https://doi.org/10.1080/13617672.2023.2228157.

2. Eckhard Frick et al., "Do Self-Efficacy Expectation and Spirituality Provide a Buffer Against Stress-Associated Impairment of Health? A Comprehensive Analysis of the German Pastoral Ministry Study," *Journal of Religion and Health* 55, no. 2 (2016): 462, https://doi.org/10.1007/s10943–015–0040–7.

3. Arndt Büssing et al., "Spiritual Dryness as a Measure of a Specific Spiritual Crisis in Catholic Priests: Associations with Symptoms of Burnout and Distress," *Evidence-Based Complementary & Alternative Medicine* 2013 (2013): 1–10, https://doi.org/10.1155/2013/246797. Parts of this section in the book were adapted from Charles Stone, "What to Look for in a Good Friend," February 7, 2024, https://charlesstone.com/look-good-friend/.

4. Bertha Chambers, *Oswald Chambers: His Life and Work* (Eugene, OR: Wipf and Stock, 2017), 78.

5. Brittany Proffitt, "The Puritans and Spiritual Dryness: Hope in God and His Word," *So We Speak*, June 10, 2022, https://www.sowespeak.com/post/the-puritans-and-spiritual-dryness-hope-in-god-and-his-word.

6. Jonathan M Golden et al., "Spirituality and Burnout: An Incremental Validity Study," *Journal of Psychology & Theology* 32, no. 2 (2004): 115–25, https://doi.org/10.1177/009164710403200204.

7. Diane J. Chandler, "The Impact of Pastor's Spiritual Practices on Burnout," *The Journal of Pastoral Care & Counseling* 64, no. 2 (2010), https://doi.org/10.1177/154230501006400206.

8. Thomas V. Frederick et al., "Burnout in Christian Perspective," *Pastoral Psychology* 67, no. 3 (2018): 267, https://doi.org/10.1007/s11089–017–0799–4.

9. Dara G. Friedman-Wheeler et al., "Do Mood-Regulation Expectancies for Coping Strategies Predict Their Use? A Daily Diary Study," *International Journal of Stress Management* 26, no. 3 (2019): 287–96, https://doi.org/10.1037/str0000115.

10. Ulrich Kirk and Johanne L. Axelsen, "Heart Rate Variability Is Enhanced During Mindfulness Practice: A Randomized Controlled Trial Involving a 10-Day Online-Based Mindfulness Intervention," *PLOS ONE* 15, no. 12 (2020): e0243488, https://doi.org/10.1371/journal.pone.0243488.

11. Daniela Rodrigues de Oliveira et al., "Mindfulness Meditation Training Effects on Quality of Life, Immune Function and Glutathione Metabolism in Service Healthy Female Teachers: A Randomized Pilot Clinical Trial," *Brain, Behavior, and Immunity—Health* 18 (2021): 100372, https://doi.org/10.1016/j.bbih.2021.100372.

12. Marta J. Kadziolka et al., "Trait-Like Mindfulness Promotes Healthy Self-Regulation of Stress," *Mindfulness* 7 (2015), https://doi.org/10.1007/s12671–015–0437–0.

13. Melissa A. Rosenkranz et al., "A Comparison of Mindfulness-Based Stress Reduction and an Active Control in Modulation of Neurogenic Inflammation," *Brain, Behavior, and Immunity* 27 (2013): 174–84, https://doi.org/10.1016/j.bbi.2012.10.013.

14. Grant R. Bickerton et al., "Spiritual Resources as Antecedents of Clergy Well-Being: The Importance of Occupationally Specific Variables," *Journal of Vocational Behavior* 87 (2015): 123, https://doi.org/10.1016/j.jvb.2015.01.002.

15. Jeffrey M. Greeson et al., "Changes in Spirituality Partly Explain Health-Related Quality of Life Outcomes after Mindfulness-Based Stress Reduction," *Journal of Behavioral Medicine* 34, no. 6 (2011): 508, https://doi.org/10.1007/s10865–011–9332-x.

16. Katheryn Rhoads Meek et al., "Maintaining Personal Resiliency: Lessons Learned from Evangelical Protestant Clergy," *Journal of Psychology & Theology* 31, no. 4 (2003): 339–47, https://doi.org/10.1177/009164710303100404; Christopher G. Ellison et al., "Religious Resources, Spiritual Struggles, and Mental Health in a Nationwide Sample of PCUSA Clergy," *Pastoral Psychology* 59, no. 3 (June 2010): 300, https://doi.org/10.1007/s11089–009–0239–1; Maureen H. Miner et al., "Ministry Orientation and Ministry Outcomes: Evaluation of a New Multidimensional Model of Clergy Burnout and Job Satisfaction," *Journal of Occupational & Organizational Psychology* 83, no. 1 (2010): 169–70, https://doi.org/10.1348/096317909X414214.

17. Carol Anderson Darling et al., "Understanding Stress and Quality of Life for Clergy and Clergy Spouses," *Stress & Health: Journal of the International Society for the Investigation of Stress* 20, no. 5 (2004): 261–77, https://doi.org/10.1002/smi.1031.

18. Shauna L. Shapiro et al., "Mindfulness-Based Stress Reduction Effects on Moral Reasoning and Decision Making," *The Journal of Positive Psychology* 7, no. 6 (2012): 504–15, https://doi.org/10.1080/17439760.2012.723732.

19. Maureen H. Miner, "Burnout in the First Year of Ministry: Personality and Belief Style as Important Predictors," *Mental Health, Religion & Culture* 10, no. 1 (2007): 17–29, https://doi.org/10.1080/13694670500378017.

20. Dallas Willard and Gary Black, *Renewing the Christian Mind: Essays, Interviews, and Talks* (New York: HarperOne, 2016), 31.

21. Kenneth I. Pargament, "Religion and the Problem-Solving Process: Three Styles of Coping," *Journal for the Scientific Study of Religion* 27, no. 1 (1988): 90–104, https://doi.org/10.2307/1387404.

22. Pargament, "Religion."

23. Jane K. Ferguson et al., "Centering Prayer as a Healing Response to Everyday Stress: A Psychological and Spiritual Process," *Pastoral Psychology* 59, no. 3 (2010): 314, https://doi .org/10.1007/s11089–009–0225–7.

24. Grant R. Bickerton et al., "Spiritual Resources and Work Engagement among Religious Workers: A Three-Wave Longitudinal Study," *Journal of Occupational and Organizational Psychology* 87, no. 2 (2014): 371, https://doi.org/10.1111/joop.12052.

25. Kenneth Pargament et al., "The Brief RCOPE: Current Psychometric Status of a Short Measure of Religious Coping," *Religions* 2, no. 1 (2011): 51–76 https://doi.org/10.3390/rel2010051.

26. Michiel van Elk et al., "The Neural Correlates of the Awe Experience: Reduced Default Mode Network Activity During Feelings of Awe," *Human Brain Mapping* 40, no. 12 (2019): 3561, https://doi.org/10.1002/hbm.24616.

27. Yang Bai et al., "Awe, Daily Stress, and Elevated Life Satisfaction," *Journal of Personality and Social Psychology* 120, no. 4 (2021): 853, https://doi.org/10.1037/pspa0000267.

28. Jennifer E. Stellar et al., "Positive Affect and Markers of Inflammation: Discrete Positive Emotions Predict Lower Levels of Inflammatory Cytokines," *Emotion* 15, no. 2 (2015): 129–33, https://doi.org/10.1037/emo0000033.

29. David Furman et al., "Chronic Inflammation in the Etiology of Disease Across the Life Span," *Nature Medicine* 25, no. 12 (2019): 1822–32, https://doi.org/10.1038/s41591–019–0675–0.

30. Ethan Kross, *Chatter: The Voice in Our Head, Why It Matters, and How to Harness It* (New York: Crown, 2021), 119.

31. Kross, *Chatter*, 146.

32. Luisa J. Gallagher, "A Theology of Rest: Sabbath Principles for Ministry," *Christian Education Journal* 16, no. 1 (2019): 139, https://doi.org/10.1177/0739891318821124.

33. Gallagher, "Theology of Rest," 141.

34. Christina Maslach, *Burnout: The Cost of Caring* (Englewood Cliffs, NJ: Malor Books, 2011); Jonathan Whiting, "Spiritual Well-Being as a Mediator in the Relationship Between Spiritual Behavior and Emotional Exhaustion in Pastors" (PhD diss., Northwestern University, 2017), https://archives.northwestu.edu/handle/nu/25239.

35. Holly Hough et al., "Relationships Between Sabbath Observance and Mental, Physical, and Spiritual Health in Clergy," *Pastoral Psychology* 68, no. 2 (2019): 171–93, https://doi .org/10.1007/s11089–018–0838–9.

36. Gallagher, "Theology of Rest," 144.

37. Hough et al., "Relationships Between Sabbath Observance."

38. Wayne Muller, *Sabbath: Restoring the Sacred Rhythm of Rest* (New York: Bantam, 1999), 82–83.

39. Michael E. Kerr and Murray Bowen, *Family Evaluation: An Approach Based on Bowen Theory* (New York: Norton, 1988).

40. Kerr and Bowen, *Family Evaluation*.

41. Scott Dunbar et al., "Calling, Caring, and Connecting: Burnout in Christian Ministry," *Mental Health, Religion & Culture* 23, no. 2 (2020): 173–86, https://doi.org/10.1080/136746 76.2020.1744548.

42. Dunbar et al., "Calling," 181.

43. J. David Creswell et al., "Affirmation of Personal Values Buffers Neuroendocrine and Psychological Stress Responses," *Psychological Science* 16, no. 11 (2005): 846–51, https://doi .org/10.1111/j.1467–9280.2005.01624.x.

44. Kelly McGonigal, *The Upside of Stress: Why Stress Is Good for You, and How to Get Good at It* (New York: Avery, 2015), 70.

## CHAPTER 9: PRACTICE 6: CULTIVATE CERTAINTY

1. Michel J. Dugas and Melisa Robichaud, *Cognitive-Behavioral Treatment for Generalized Anxiety Disorder: From Science to Practice* (New York: Routledge, 2007).

2. Kelly McGonigal, *The Upside of Stress: Why Stress Is Good for You, and How to Get Good at It* (New York: Avery, 2015), 17.

3. Joshua J. Knabb and Veola E. Vazquez, "A Randomized Controlled Trial of a 2-Week Internet-Based Contemplative Prayer Program for Christians with Daily Stress," *Spirituality in Clinical Practice* 5, no. 1 (2018): 37–53, https://doi.org/10.1037/scp0000154.

4. Oliver Burkeman, *Four Thousand Weeks: Time Management for Mortals* (New York: Farrar, Straus and Giroux, 2021), Kindle, loc. 1341.

5. Joshua J. Knabb et al., "Surrendering to God's Providence: A Three-Part Study on Providence-Focused Therapy for Recurrent Worry (PFT-RW)," *Psychology of Religion and Spirituality* 9, no. 2 (2017): 186, https://doi.org/10.1037/rel0000081.

6. G. R. Hockey, "Compensatory Control in the Regulation of Human Performance Under Stress and High Workload; a Cognitive-Energetical Framework," *Biological Psychology* 45, nos. 1–3 (1997): 73–93, https://doi.org/10.1016/s0301-0511(96)05223-4.

7. Aaron C. Kay et al., "God and the Government: Testing a Compensatory Control Mechanism for the Support of External Systems," *Journal of Personality and Social Psychology* 95, no. 1 (2008): 18–35, https://doi.org/10.1037/0022-3514.95.1.18.

8. Oswald Chambers, *My Utmost for His Highest*, rev. ed. (Grand Rapids, MI: Discovery House Publishers, 1992), 120.

9. Achim Peters et al., "Uncertainty and Stress: Why It Causes Diseases and How It Is Mastered by the Brain," *Progress in Neurobiology* 156 (2017): 164–88, https://doi.org/10.1016/j.pneurobio.2017.05.004.

10. Amishi P. Jha, *Peak Mind: Find Your Focus, Own Your Attention, Invest 12 Minutes a Day* (New York: HarperOne, 2021), 54–55.

11. Ming Hsu et al., "Neural Systems Responding to Degrees of Uncertainty in Human Decision-Making," *Science* 310, no. 5754 (2005): 1680–83, https://doi.org/10.1126/science.1115327.

12. Srinivasan S. Pilay, *Your Brain and Business: The Neuroscience of Great Leaders* (Upper Saddle River, NJ: FT Press, 2011), Kindle, loc. 4110.

13. Michael L. Platt and Scott A. Huettel, "Risky Business: The Neuroeconomics of Decision Making Under Uncertainty," *Nature Neuroscience* 11, no. 4 (2008): 398–403, https://doi.org/10.1038/nn2062.

14. Trey Hedden and John D. E. Gabrieli, "The Ebb and Flow of Attention in the Human Brain," *Nature Neuroscience* 9, no. 7 (2006): 863–65, https://doi.org/10.1038/nn0706-863.

15. Cyril Herry et al., "Processing of Temporal Unpredictability in Human and Animal Amygdala," *The Journal of Neuroscience* 27, no. 22 (2007): 5958–66, https://doi.org/10.1523/JNEUROSCI.5218-06.2007.

16. Kristen D. Petagna and Jolie B. Wormwood, "Who Can Predict Their Future Feelings? Individual Differences in Affective Forecasting Accuracy," *Social Psychological and Personality Science* (2023): https://doi.org/10.1177/19485506231208749.

17. J. Bomyea et al., "Intolerance of Uncertainty as a Mediator of Reductions in Worry in a Cognitive Behavioral Treatment Program for Generalized Anxiety Disorder," *Journal of Anxiety Disorders* 33 (2015): 90–94, https://doi.org/10.1016/j.janxdis.2015.05.004.

18. Bomyea et al, "Intolerance."

19. Máire B. Ford and Nancy L. Collins, "Self-Esteem Moderates Neuroendocrine and Psychological Responses to Interpersonal Rejection," *Journal of Personality and Social Psychology* 98, no. 3 (2010): 405–19, https://doi.org/10.1037/a0017345.

20. Mansoor Alimehdi et al., "The Effectiveness of Mindfulness-Based Stress Reduction on Intolerance of Uncertainty and Anxiety Sensitivity among Individuals with Generalized Anxiety Disorder," *Asian Social Science* 12 (2016): 179, https://doi.org/10.5539/ass.v12n4p179.

21. Erika Garcia-Klemas, "Comparing the Efficacy of a Centering or Intercessory Prayer Intervention on Stress in Christian Participants" (PhD diss., Northcentral University, 2019), ProQuest (22588942).

22. Douglas W. Turton and Leslie J. Francis, "The Relationship Between Attitude Toward Prayer and Professional Burnout Among Anglican Parochial Clergy in England: Are Praying Clergy

Healthier Clergy?," *Mental Health*, Religion & Culture 10, no. 1 (2007): 61–74, https://doi.org/10.1080/13674670601012246.

23. Lorri Castro, "Prospective Relationships Among Types of Prayer, Trauma, Perceived Stress and Physical Health" (PhD diss, Loma Linda University, 2014), ProQuest (3721148).
24. Jane K. Ferguson et al., "Centering Prayer as a Healing Response to Everyday Stress: A Psychological and Spiritual Process," *Pastoral Psychology* 59, no. 3 (2010): 305–29, https://doi.org/10.1007/s11089–009–0225–7.
25. Ferguson et al., "Centering Prayer," 318.
26. Ferguson et al., "Centering Prayer," 313.
27. Father Jean Baptiste Saint-Jure and Blessed Claude de la Colombière, *Trustful Surrender to Divine Providence: The Secret of Peace and Happiness*, trans. Paul Garvin (Charlotte, NC: TAN Books, 1984).
28. Knabb et al., "Surrendering," 182.
29. Knabb et al., "Surrendering," 186.
30. Knabb et al., "Surrendering," 186–87.
31. Knabb and Vazquez, "Randomized Controlled Trial," 40.
32. Ferguson et al, "Centering Prayer," 313.
33. Leslie J. Francis, "Healthy Leadership: The Science of Clergy Work-Related Psychological Health. Edited Collection," in *The Future of Lived Religious Leadership*, ed. Rein Brouwer (Amsterdam: VU University Press, 2018), 116–34.
34. Castro, "Prospective Relationships."
35. Castro, "Prospective Relationships."
36. Lisa Tams, "Journaling to Reduce COVID-19 Stress," MSU Extension, November 11, 2020, https://www.canr.msu.edu/news/journaling_to_reduce_stress.
37. Castro, "Prospective Relationships."

## CHAPTER 10: PRACTICE 7: GROW GRATITUDE

1. Amit Sood, *SMART with Dr. Sood: The Four-Module Stress Management And Resilience Training Program* (Rochester, MN: Global Center for Resiliency and Wellbeing, 2019), 170.
2. Sood, *SMART*.
3. Da Jiang, "Feeling Gratitude Is Associated with Better Well-Being Across the Life Span: A Daily Diary Study During the COVID-19 Outbreak," *The Journals of Gerontology: Series B* 77, no. 4 (2022): e36–45, https://doi.org/10.1093/geronb/gbaa220.
4. Marcus Kilian, "Wesleyan Leadership Formation: A Neuroscience Integration," *Journal of Psychology & Christianity* 38, no. 4 (2019): 253–67.
5. "Can Gratitude Increase Quality of Life?," Penn Medicine Princeton Health, November 22, 2022, https://www.princetonhcs.org/about-princeton-health/news-and-information/news/can-gratitude-increase-quality-of-life.
6. Marta Jackowska et al., "The Impact of a Brief Gratitude Intervention on Subjective Well-Being, Biology and Sleep," *Journal of Health Psychology* 21, no. 10 (2016): 2207–17, https://doi.org/10.1177/1359105315572455.
7. Sara B. Algoe et al., "Oxytocin and Social Bonds: The Role of Oxytocin in Perceptions of Romantic Partners' Bonding Behavior," *Psychological Science* 28, no. 12 (2017): 1763, https://doi.org/10.1177/0956797617716922.
8. C. Nathan DeWall et al., "A Grateful Heart Is a Nonviolent Heart: Cross-Sectional, Experience Sampling, Longitudinal, and Experimental Evidence," *Social Psychological and Personality Science* 3, no. 2 (2012): 232–40, https://doi.org/10.1177/1948550611416675.
9. Madhuleena Chowdhury, "The Neuroscience of Gratitude and How It Affects Anxiety & Grief," PositivePsychology.com, April 9, 2019, https://positivepsychology.com/neuroscience-of-gratitude/.
10. Chowdhury, "Neuroscience of Gratitude."
11. Laura I. Hazlett et al., "Exploring Neural Mechanisms of the Health Benefits of Gratitude in Women: A Randomized Controlled Trial," *Brain, Behavior, and Immunity* 95 (2021): 444–53, https://doi.org/10.1016/j.bbi.2021.04.019.

12. Yu Komase et al., "Effects of Gratitude Intervention on Mental Health and Wellbeing among Workers: A Systematic Review," *Journal of Occupational Health* 63, no. 1 (2021): e12290, https://doi.org/10.1002/1348–9585.12290.
13. Randolph W. Shipon, "Gratitude: Effect on Perspectives and Blood Pressure of Inner-City African-American Hypertensive Patients," (PhD diss., Temple University, 2007).
14. Rachel A. Millstein et al., "The Effects of Optimism and Gratitude on Adherence, Functioning and Mental Health Following an Acute Coronary Syndrome," *General Hospital Psychiatry* 43 (2016): 17–22, https://doi.org/10.1016/j.genhosppsych.2016.08.006.
15. Robert A. Emmons and Michael E. McCullough, "Counting Blessings Versus Burdens: An Experimental Investigation of Gratitude and Subjective Well-Being in Daily Life," *Journal of Personality and Social Psychology* 84, no. 2 (2003): 377–89, https://doi.org/10.1037/0022–3514.84.2.377.
16. Sood, *SMART*, 73.
17. Prathik Kini et al., "The Effects of Gratitude Expression on Neural Activity," *NeuroImage* 128 (2016): 1–10, https://doi.org/10.1016/j.neuroimage.2015.12.040.
18. Joyce E. Bono et al., "Building Positive Resources: Effects of Positive Events and Positive Reflection on Work Stress and Health," *Academy of Management Journal* 56, no. 6 (2013): 1619, https://doi.org/10.5465/amj.2011.0272.
19. Cameron Lee, "Dispositional Resiliency and Adjustment in Protestant Pastors: A Pilot Study," *Pastoral Psychology* 59, no. 5 (2010): 631–40, https://doi.org/10.1007/s11089–010–0283-x.
20. Christopher Bergland, "4 Reasons Writing Things Down on Paper Still Reigns Supreme," *Psychology Today*, March 19, 2021, https://www.psychologytoday.com/us/blog/the-athletes-way/202103/4-reasons-writing-things-down-paper-still-reigns-supreme.
21. Bono et al., "Building Positive Resources."
22. Bono et al., "Building Positive Resources," 1605.
23. Erin M. Fekete and Nathan T. Deichert, "A Brief Gratitude Writing Intervention Decreased Stress and Negative Affect During the COVID-19 Pandemic," *Journal of Happiness Studies* 23, no. 6 (2022): 2427–48, https://doi.org/10.1007/s10902–022–00505–6.
24. Joanna Collicutt and Roger Bretherton, *Being Mindful, Being Christian: A Guide to Mindful Discipleship* (Oxford: Monarch Books, 2016), 190.
25. Patrick L. Hill et al., "Examining the Pathways between Gratitude and Self-Rated Physical Health across Adulthood," *Personality and Individual Differences* 54, no. 1 (2013): 92–96, https://doi.org/10.1016/j.paid.2012.08.011.
26. Sood, *SMART*, 173.
27. Sood, *SMART*, 173.
28. Annie Regan et al., "Are Some Ways of Expressing Gratitude More Beneficial Than Others? Results From a Randomized Controlled Experiment," *Affective Science* 4, no. 1 (2023): 72–81, https://doi.org/10.1007/s42761–022–00160–3.
29. Wynne Parry and LiveScience, "'Gratitude' Map Invites Users to Accentuate the Positive," *Scientific American*, January 2, 2013, https://www.scientificamerican.com/article/gratitude-map-invites-use/.
30. Steven M. Southwick and Dennis S. Charney, *Resilience: The Science of Mastering Life's Greatest Challenges*, 2nd ed. (Cambridge: Cambridge University Press, 2018), 46.
31. Edward C. Chang, ed., *Optimism & Pessimism: Implications for Theory, Research, and Practice* (Washington, DC: American Psychological Association, 2001).
32. Sood, *SMART*, 173.

## CHAPTER 11: PRACTICE 8: SAFEGUARD SAFETY

1. Amy Gallo, "What Is Psychological Safety?" *Harvard Business Review*, February 15, 2023, https://hbr.org/2023/02/what-is-psychological-safety.
2. T. Scott Bledsoe and Kimberly A. Setterlund, "Thriving in Ministry: Exploring the Support Systems and Self-Care Practices of Experienced Pastors," *Journal of Family and Community*

*Ministries* 28 (2015): 48–66; Rae Jean Proeschold-Bell, et al., "The Glory of God Is a Human Being Fully Alive: Predictors of Positive Versus Negative Mental Health Among Clergy," *Journal for the Scientific Study of Religion* 54, no. 4 (2015): 702–21, https://doi.org/10.1111/jssr.12234.

3. Charles Stone, *Every Pastor's First 180 Days: How to Start and Stay Strong in a New Church Job* (Equip Press, 2019), 38–39. Adapted with permission.

4. Stephen W. Porges, "Neuroception: A Subconscious System for Detecting Threats and Safety," *Zero to Three* 24, no. 5 (2004): 19–24.

5. Julianne Holt-Lunstad et al., "Social Relationships and Mortality Risk: A Meta-Analytic Review," *PLOS Medicine* 7, no. 7 (2010): 1–20, https://doi.org/10.1371/journal.pmed.1000316.

6. Stephanie M. Sherman et al., "Social Support, Stress and the Aging Brain," *Social Cognitive and Affective Neuroscience* 11, no. 7 (2016): 1050–58, https://doi.org/10.1093/scan/nsv071.

7. Naomi I. Eisenberger, "The Neural Bases of Social Pain: Evidence for Shared Representations with Physical Pain," *Psychosomatic Medicine* 74, no. 2 (2012): 126–35, https://doi.org/10.1097/PSY.0b013e3182464dd1.

8. Kelly McGonigal, *The Upside of Stress: Why Stress Is Good for You, and How to Get Good at It* (New York: Avery, 2015), 49.

9. Dan Buettner and Sam Skemp, "Blue Zones," *American Journal of Lifestyle Medicine* 10, no. 5 (2016): 318–21, https://doi.org/10.1177/1559827616637066.

10. Golnaz Tabibnia and Dan Radecki, "Resilience Training That Can Change the Brain," *Consulting Psychology Journal: Practice and Research* 70, no. 1 (2018): 59–88, https://doi.org/10.1037/cpb0000110.

11. Timothy D. Wilson, *Strangers to Ourselves: Discovering the Adaptive Unconscious* (Cambridge, MA: Belknap Press, 2004).

12. Wilson, *Strangers*.

13. Dan Radecki et al., *Psychological Safety: The Key to Happy, High-Performing People and Teams* (Orange County, CA: The Academy of Brain-Based Leadership, 2018), 29.

14. Evian Gordon et al., "An 'Integrative Neuroscience' Platform: Application to Profiles of Negativity and Positivity Bias," *Journal of Integrative Neuroscience* 7, no. 3 (2008): 345–66, https://doi.org/10.1142/S0219635208001927.

15. Jos F. Brosschot et al., "Generalized Unsafety Theory of Stress: Unsafe Environments and Conditions, and the Default Stress Response," *International Journal of Environmental Research and Public Health* 15, no. 3 (2018): 464, https://doi.org/10.3390/ijerph15030464.

16. Jessica R. Cohen et al., "Intentional and Incidental Self-Control in Ventrolateral Prefrontal Cortext," in *Principles of Frontal Lobe Function*, 2nd ed., eds. Donalt T. Stuss and Robert T. Knight (New York: Oxford University Press, 2013), 417–40.

17. Ethan Kross, *Chatter: The Voice in Our Head, Why It Matters, and How to Harness It* (New York: Crown, 2021), Kindle, loc. 1616.

18. James Fowler and Nicholas Christakis, "Dynamic Spread of Happiness in a Large Social Network: Longitudinal Analysis Over 20 Years in the Framingham Heart Study," *BMJ* 337 (2008): a2338, https://doi.org/10.1136/bmj.a2338.

19. Leonard Mlodinow, *Emotional: How Feelings Shape Our Thinking* (New York: Pantheon, 2022), 186.

20. Thomas Baumgartner et al., "Oxytocin Shapes the Neural Circuitry of Trust and Trust Adaptation in Humans," *Neuron* 58, no. 4 (2008): 639–50, https://doi.org/10.1016/j.neuron.2008.04.009.

21. Cyndi Bennett, "CPTSD in the Workplace: Psychological Safety," CPTSD Foundation, March 16, 2023, https://cptsdfoundation.org/2023/03/16/cptsd-in-the-workplace-psychological-safety/.

22. Kross, *Chatter*, 93.

23. Stone, *Every Pastor's First 180 Days*, 38–39. Material adapted by permission.

## CHAPTER 12: PRACTICE 9: SLEEP SMART

1. Anna Fleck, "Four in Ten Italians Can't Sleep," *Statista*, December 18, 2023, https://www
.statista.com/chart/29517/share-of-adults-that-have-trouble-sleeping.
2. Cynthia Reuben et al., "Sleep Medication Use in Adults Aged 18 and Over: United States,
2020," National Center for Health Statistics Data Brief, No. 462, January 2023, https://www
.cdc.gov/nchs/data/databriefs/db462.pdf.
3. Daniel F. Kripke, "Surprising View of Insomnia and Sleeping Pills," *Sleep* 36, no. 8 (2013):
1127–8, https://doi.org/10.5665/sleep.2868; Matthew D. Mitchell et al., "Comparative
Effectiveness of Cognitive Behavioral Therapy for Insomnia: A Systematic Review," *BMC
Family Practice* 13 (2012): 40, https://doi.org/10.1186/1471–2296–13–40.
4. Vijay Kumar Chattu et al., "The Global Problem of Insufficient Sleep and Its Serious
Public Health Implications," *Healthcare* 7, no. 1 (2018): 1, https://doi.org/10.3390/
healthcare7010001.
5. Chattu et al., "Global Problem."
6. Steven W. Lockley and Russell G. Foster, *Sleep: A Very Short Introduction* (New York: Oxford
University Press, 2012), 26.
7. Munish Goyal and Jeremy Johnson, "Obstructive Sleep Apnea Diagnosis and Management,"
*Missouri Medicine* 114, no. 2 (2017): 120–24.
8. "Medical Education," Harvard Medical School Division of Sleep Medicine, 2023, https://
sleep.hms.harvard.edu/education-training/medical-education.
9. Andrew Bishop, *Theosomnia: A Christian Theology of Sleep* (London: Jessica Kingsley Publishers,
2018).
10. D. A. Carson, *Scandalous: The Cross and Resurrection of Jesus* (Wheaton, IL: Crossway, 2010),
147.
11. Per Kristian Eide et al., "Sleep Deprivation Impairs Molecular Clearance from the Human
Brain," *Brain* 144, no. 3 (2021): 863–74, https://doi.org/10.1093/brain/awaa443.
12. Robert Stickgold and Matthew P. Walker, "Sleep-Dependent Memory Consolidation and
Reconsolidation," *Sleep Medicine* 8, no. 4 (2007): 331–43, https://doi.org/10.1016/j.sleep
.2007.03.011.
13. Stanislas Dehaene, *How We Learn: Why Brains Learn Better Than Any Machine . . . for Now*
(New York: Viking, 2020), 90, 231.
14. Greer S. Kirshenbaum et al., "Adult-Born Neurons Maintain Hippocampal Cholinergic Inputs
and Support Working Memory During Aging," *Molecular Psychiatry* 28 (2023): July 21,
5337–5349, https://doi.org/10.1038/s41380–023–02167-z.
15. Anka D. Mueller et al., "Sleep and Adult Neurogenesis: Implications for Cognition and
Mood," *Current Topics in Behavioral Neurosciences* 25 (2015): 151–81, https://doi.org/
10.1007/7854_2013_251.
16. Benjamin C. Storm, "The Benefit of Forgetting in Thinking and Remembering," *Current
Directions in Psychological Science* 20, no. 5 (2011): 291–95.
17. "Sleep's Crucial Role in Preserving Memory," Yale School of Medicine, last updated May 10,
2022, https://medicine.yale.edu/news-article/sleeps-crucial-role-in-preserving-memory/.
18. R. D. Cartwright et al., "Broken Dreams: A Study of the Effects of Divorce and Depression on
Dream Content," *Psychiatry* 47, no. 3 (1984): 251–59, https://doi.org/10.1080/00332747.198
4.11024246.
19. Heather A. Mitchell and David Weinshenker, "Good Night and Good Luck: Norepinephrine
in Sleep Pharmacology," *Biochemical Pharmacology* 79, no. 6 (2010): 801–9, https://doi
.org/10.1016/j.bcp.2009.10.004.
20. Andrea N. Goldstein-Piekarski et al., "Sleep Deprivation Impairs the Human Central and
Peripheral Nervous System Discrimination of Social Threat," *Journal of Neuroscience* 35,
no. 28 (2015): 10135–45, https://doi.org/10.1523/JNEUROSCI.5254–14.2015.
21. Eide et al., "Sleep Deprivation."

22. K. E. Demos et al., "Partial Sleep Deprivation Impacts Impulsive Action but Not Impulsive Decision-Making," *Physiology & Behavior* 164 (Pt. A) (2016): 214–19, https://doi.org/10.1016/j.physbeh.2016.06.003.

23. Sergio Garbarino et al., "Role of Sleep Deprivation in Immune-Related Disease Risk and Outcomes," *Communications Biology* 4 (2021): 1304, https://doi.org/10.1038/s42003–021–02825–4.

24. Matthew Walker, *Why We Sleep: Unlocking the Power of Sleep and Dreams* (New York: Scribner, 2017), 132.

25. Susan Hagen, "The Mind's Eye," *Rochester Review* 74, no. 4 (2012): 6, https://www.rochester.edu/pr/Review/V74N4/pdf/0402_brainscience.pdf.

26. All images in this chapter generated by DALL-E, OpenAI, October 20, 2023.

27. Marnin Romm et al., "A Meta-Analysis of Therapeutic Pain Neuroscience Education, Using Dosage and Treatment Format as Moderator Variables," *Pain Practice* 21, no. 3 (2020): 366–80, https://doi.org/10.1111/papr.12962.

28. Ellen P. Lukens and William R. McFarlane, "Psychoeducation as Evidence-Based Practice: Considerations for Practice, Research, and Policy," *Brief Treatment and Crisis Intervention* 4, no. 3 (2004): 205–25, https://doi.org/10.1093/brief-treatment/mhh019.

29. Nathaniel F. Watson et al., "Recommended Amount of Sleep for a Healthy Adult: A Joint Consensus Statement of the American Academy of Sleep Medicine and Sleep Research Society," *Journal of Clinical Sleep Medicine* 11, no. 06 (2015): 591–92, https://doi.org/10.5664/jcsm.4758.

30. Shingo Kitamura et al., "Estimating Individual Optimal Sleep Duration and Potential Sleep Debt," *Scientific Reports* 6 (2016): 35812, https://doi.org/10.1038/srep35812.

31. Ya Chai et al., "Two Nights of Recovery Sleep Restores Hippocampal Connectivity but Not Episodic Memory after Total Sleep Deprivation," *Scientific Reports* 10, no. 1 (2020): 8774, https://doi.org/10.1038/s41598–020–65086-x.

32. "Blue Light Has a Dark Side," Harvard Health Publishing, July 24, 2024, https://www.health.harvard.edu/staying-healthy/blue-light-has-a-dark-side.

33. Miranda M. Lim et al., "Sleep Deprivation Differentially Affects Dopamine Receptor Subtypes in Mouse Striatum," *Neuroreport* 22, no. 10 (2011): 489–93, https://doi.org/10.1097/WNR.0b013e32834846a0.

34. Anthony R. Stenson et al., "Total Sleep Deprivation Reduces Top-down Regulation of Emotion Without Altering Bottom-up Affective Processing," *PLOS ONE* 16, no. 9 (2021): e0256983, https://doi.org/10.1371/journal.pone.0256983.

35. Amir Qaseem et al., "Management of Chronic Insomnia Disorder in Adults: A Clinical Practice Guideline From the American College of Physicians," *Annals of Internal Medicine* 165, no. 2 (2016): 125–33, https://doi.org/10.7326/M15–2175.

36. Cheng Zhang et al., "Digital Cognitive Behavioral Therapy for Insomnia Using a Smartphone Application in China: A Pilot Randomized Clinical Trial," *JAMA Network Open* 6, no. 3 (2023): e234866, https://doi.org/10.1001/jamanetworkopen.2023.4866.

37. Danielle Pacheco and Abhinav Singh, "STOP-Bang Score and Obstructive Sleep Apnea," *Sleep Foundation*, last updated December 22, 2023, https://www.sleepfoundation.org/sleep-apnea/stop-bang-score.

38. Gregg Jacobs and Richard Friedman, "EEG Spectral Analysis of Relaxation Techniques," *Applied Psychophysiology and Biofeedback* 29 (2005): 245–54, https://doi.org/10.1007/s10484–004–0385–2.

39. L. Baillargeon et al., "Stimulus-Control: Nonpharmacologic Treatment for Insomnia," *Canadian Family Physician* 44 (1998): 73–79.

40. Laura Palagini et al., "Sleep-Related Cognitive Processes, Arousal, and Emotion Dysregulation in Insomnia Disorder: The Role of Insomnia-Specific Rumination," *Sleep Medicine* 30 (2017): 97–104, https://doi.org/10.1016/j.sleep.2016.11.004.